Cooking Danish
A Taste of Denmark

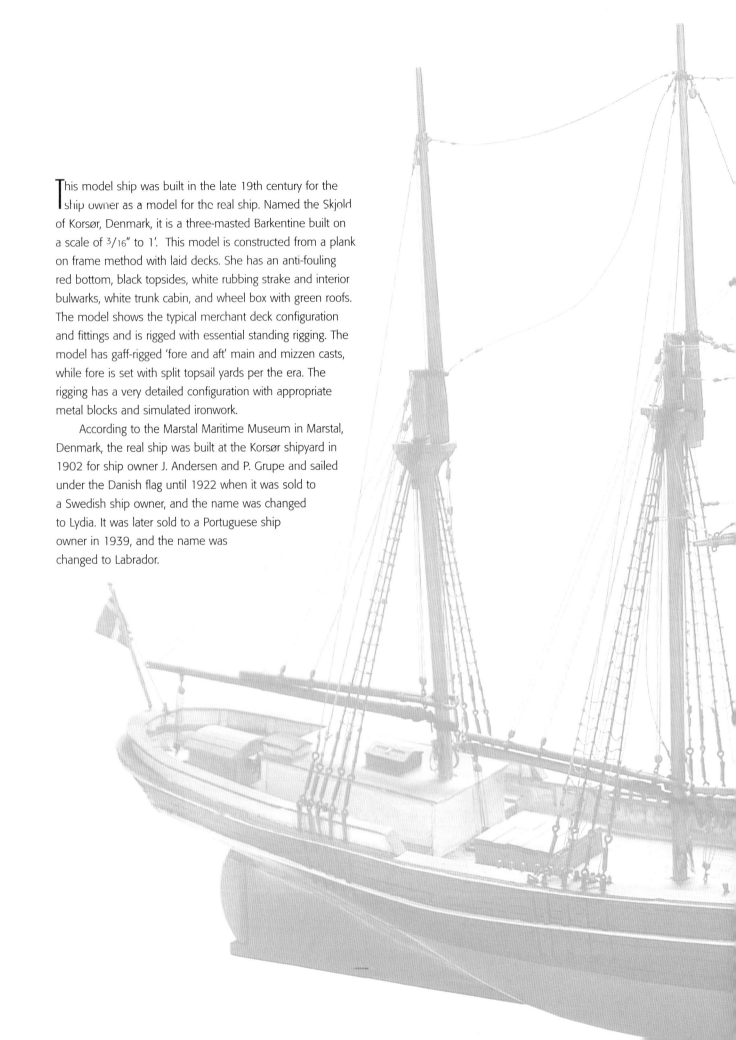

This model ship was built in the late 19th century for the ship owner as a model for the real ship. Named the Skjold of Korsør, Denmark, it is a three-masted Barkentine built on a scale of $^3/_{16}$" to 1'. This model is constructed from a plank on frame method with laid decks. She has an anti-fouling red bottom, black topsides, white rubbing strake and interior bulwarks, white trunk cabin, and wheel box with green roofs. The model shows the typical merchant deck configuration and fittings and is rigged with essential standing rigging. The model has gaff-rigged 'fore and aft' main and mizzen casts, while fore is set with split topsail yards per the era. The rigging has a very detailed configuration with appropriate metal blocks and simulated ironwork.

According to the Marstal Maritime Museum in Marstal, Denmark, the real ship was built at the Korsør shipyard in 1902 for ship owner J. Andersen and P. Grupe and sailed under the Danish flag until 1922 when it was sold to a Swedish ship owner, and the name was changed to Lydia. It was later sold to a Portuguese ship owner in 1939, and the name was changed to Labrador.

Cooking Danish

by Stig Hansen
The Viking Chef

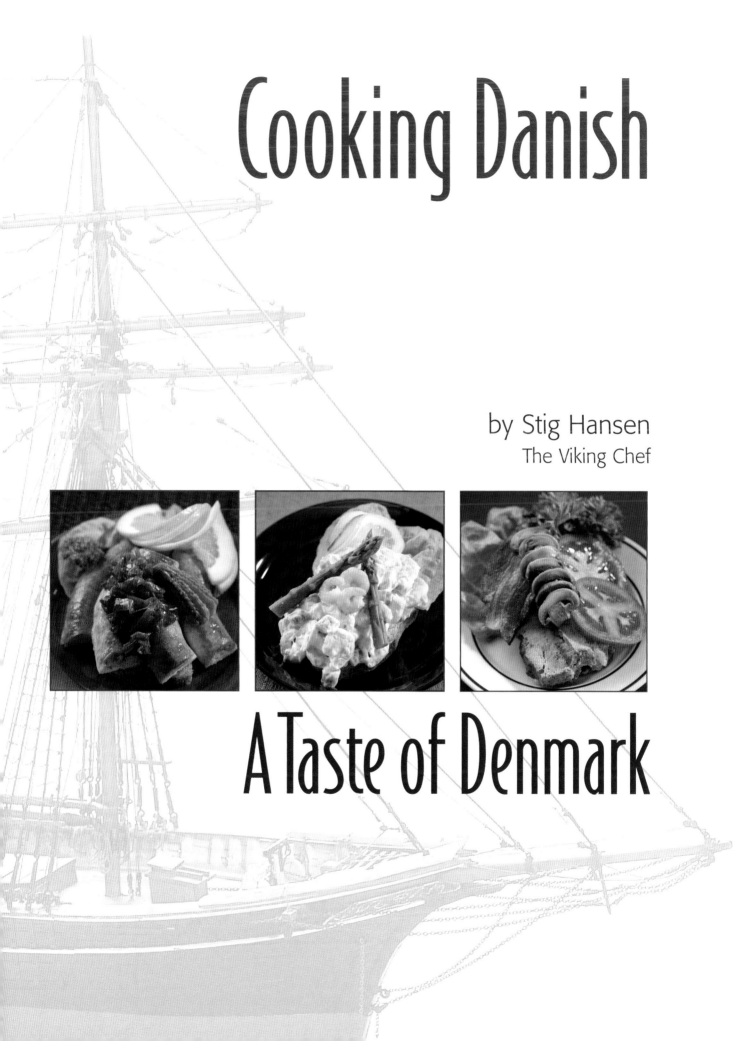

A Taste of Denmark

Cooking Danish
A Taste of Denmark

Published by Stig Hansen
Copyright © 2007
Stig Hansen
P.O. Box 930
Eden, Utah 84310
801-745-0388

Food Photography and author's photography by Curtis D. Granthen
© Stig Hansen
Food Stylist Harriett E. Granthen
Page 14 photograph © by visitdenmark.com
Pages 7, 10, 17, 57, 89, 130 photographs © by Dan Hansen

Library of Congress Number: 2006939298
ISBN: 978-0-9791019-0-8

Edited and Manufactured by
Favorite Recipes® Press
An imprint of

FRP™

P.O. Box 305142
Nashville, Tennessee 37230
1-800-358-0560

Art Direction and Book Design: Steve Newman
Project Editor: Tanis Westbrook

Manufactured in China
First Printing 2007
10,000 copies

This book is written with fond memories
of the great Danish food that my mother prepared
during my growing up years.

My parents, Gudrun & Hans C. Hansen,
on their wedding day October 10, 1948.

Foreword

When Stig Hansen asked if I would write a foreword for his new Danish cookbook, I was flattered and excited. Then apprehension set in. How could I possibly convey the beauty and deliciousness of Danish cooking? I had been the General Manager of a corporate hotel and had never visited Denmark. "Just write what you remember," Stig told me. He was our Executive Chef—European-trained—and anxious to share the mouthwatering tastes of the food of Denmark. So began six years of *Danish Week* in our country inn.

We decorated the lobby with posters of the Queen of Denmark, the mermaid in Copenhagen, and other scenic areas of the country. We removed the furniture and replaced it with Danish modern, played Danish tunes over the PA system, and the staff wore authentic Danish costumes loaned to us by the local Danes. Colorful flags of Denmark flew in prominent locations. Chef Hansen taught us a few phrases in his native language, which we mutilated with our American accents! We were now ready to start the festivities.

Who to invite? Queen Margrethe II? Of course. Her invitation was written in Danish. The ambassador in Washington D.C.? Why not? Both these prestigious people respectfully declined, but the Consulate General from Los Angeles made an appearance one year and was extremely complimentary. Our Portland Danish Consulate attended every day and stated it was the highlight of his year. The local Danish society (of which Stig had been the president) came out en masse, bringing grandma, grandpa, grandchildren, and neighbors.

The Danes are serious about their eating. No fast food; no eating on the run. One must sit and enjoy each course resolutely and with passion! Fine Danish beer with certain courses and aquavit (the Danish national drink) with others.

During the week for lunch we served the gorgeous Open-Face Sandwiches for which Denmark is famous. The presentation was as spectacular as the flavor. Even our corporate clientele expressed amazement.

On Friday and Saturday, the week culminated with a luncheon buffet fit for royalty, with Chef Hansen presiding over the preparation and arrangements. There was dish after delectable dish—from Frikadeller, to liver pâté, dill-cured salmon, to lemon pudding, almond cake, and cookies. The colors, the aromas, and the display of food was breathtaking. Several people said they had not seen such an array of their favorite dishes since leaving Denmark.

We learned the first year to schedule only one luncheon seating, as the Danes stayed all afternoon. They ate and drank and ate and drank in a convivial atmosphere. We scrambled to open a couple of banquet rooms to accommodate them all.

The food was the star of the show. Our customers oohed and aahed and made us promise to do it all again. Stig, however, was our star. With his knowledge, enthusiasm, and guidance, the staff had an incredible time during those never-to-be-forgotten weeks.

So try your hand at some of these savory recipes. You too can receive raves. How lucky we are that Stig has taken the time to create this fabulous cookbook.

Skål and happy eating!

Georgia Trapp Conn

Georgia Trapp Conn
Former General Manager
Nendel's Inn
Portland, Oregon

Acknowledgments

Der er et yndigt land, det står med brede bøge nær salten østerstrand—"There is a lovely country, it stands with wide beech woods near salty Baltic beaches…" as Adam Oehlenschläger described Denmark when he wrote the Danish national anthem in 1819. Truly it is a *lovely* land with great food and traditions, and I feel honored to be able to write *Cooking Danish,* a cookbook full of traditional Danish recipes that have been used in Denmark for generations.

But without the strong support from my wife, Sue, I would never have made it; always willing to taste and comment on my recipe development. Thank you for all your support and encouragement and for being my wife and loving me.

Mor og Far—Mom and Dad, thank you for being my parents and for all the support and knowledge you have given me. Thank you for being there so many Sunday mornings when I called you in Denmark and asked you for help with creating these recipes. Thank you for keeping me to the traditions.

Kids, thank you for all the encouragement and support; thank you for your appreciation for Danish food. I love cooking it for you. Candace, thanks for your suggestion for the subtitle.

Georgia Trapp Conn, thank you for your friendship, encouragement, and all the kind words in the Foreword.

Harriett and Curt Granthen, thank you for spending eight days at our house food styling and photographing all this food. And it seems that you really enjoyed eating it, too—these pictures are just beautiful!

Barbara Green, thank you for your great help and time in proofreading all the recipes. You really understand food.

Bryn Marlow, thank you for the great help with the sidebars. You really have a way with words.

Stevns Cliff on Zealand (Stevns Klint på Sjælland)

Thank you to Shaun Angler for the beautiful beer labels pictured on page 59.

Thank you to Bill Branch, Publishing Consultant; Julee Hicks, Communications Editor; Stephanie Williams, Publicist; Mary Cummings, Managing Editor; Steve Newman and Starletta Polster, Art Directors; Tanis Westbrook, Project Editor; and everyone at FRP for believing in this project.

My brother Dan, thank you for the beautiful pictures from Denmark, especially the one from Skælskør, the town where we were raised.

Thank you to my five brothers who have encouraged me with the writing of this book, although your wives cook great Danish food for you every day!

And thanks to my friends who have eaten and appreciated my Danish cooking, but most of all for encouraging me to write this book.

The Life of a Viking Chef

Born to Gudrun and Hans Christian Hansen July 17, 1954, Stig Hansen, named for a favorite Danish radio DJ, was the first of six sons. His early years were spent in Ringe, Denmark. When Stig was six years old, the family moved to the isle of Sealand. There they lived in a 250-year-old original Danish home, with a thatched roof, a well out front, and an outhouse in the back. At this early age Stig learned how to milk the neighbor's cows, drive the horses, and soon after, a tractor. His earliest memories are of having learned the lesson to always work diligently.

Like all Danish children Stig was raised Lutheran. Born in Denmark—born a Lutheran! Stig's parents served as Lutheran missionaries at an early point in their lives. They established a wonderful value system in which to raise their family of six boys.

His father, Hans, was a Boy Scout Master for more than fifty years. Thus, scouting played a large role in Stig's life. The camping and biking trips to Germany and Holland provided wonderful memories.

Stig was a newspaper boy in his early years. There is a Danish saying, "Start as a newspaper boy in Denmark, and become a millionaire in America!" A little later he became a grocery boy in his local grocery store. Not quite a millionaire in America yet!

When the family moved to Skælskør, Stig discovered fishing, which became a favorite pastime and a way to help put delicious food on the table. School in Skælskør was quite important to Stig, his favorite classes being accounting, geography, and cooking (home economics). Cooking soon took over as a priority of personal interest and it seemed to be the right place and the right fit for him.

Like other Danish schoolchildren, Stig completed Danish schooling at the age of sixteen. Some students finish with schooling at this age and begin working, while others go on to boarding school or a trade school. Some take an apprenticeship in their chosen trade, and others go on to a university if that seems suitable for their future occupation. Stig attended boarding school on the isle of Fyn for his advanced studies and then took an apprenticeship while in Seamans School.

After his studies, he worked at a five-star hotel in Copenhagen and on board ships in the Merchant Marines. He served and sailed between routes such as Ecuador and Japan, Hawaii and Los Angeles, down under to New Zealand, and then to Australia and back to Europe. It was a lot of hard work in the kitchen cooking for sailors with a strict and rather demanding labor union. Stig prepared three meals a day—and not just any meals. A main meal consisting of soup, fresh baked rolls, an entrée, and dessert were made from scratch for lunch. For the evening meal, Danish Smorgasbord and open-face sandwiches were served. Cooking from scratch meant cutting up a quarter of beef, half a hog, or a whole lamb, to mention just a few interesting tasks.

Going ashore in foreign lands was always an adventure, whether visiting a National Park in Australia, taking a safari in South Africa, or experiencing a trip on the Fast Train from Tokyo to Kobe in Japan. There was always a great new adventure ahead. After a summer spent as a chef in Greenland, where he took every opportunity to learn about whaling, Stig returned to the sailing life once again.

Stig served his country for the required time in the Danish Navy. During part of this time he served under NATO on a minesweeper ship in the English Channel, and then he served in the Torpedo Boat communications division cooking for the officers. While in the Danish Navy, his immigration papers were processed, and in 1976, Stig came to the United States of America.

Stig flew into Omaha, Nebraska, on a bright autumn day. His first job was as a chef at the famous "The Omaha Club." However, after weathering the worst Midwestern winter in more than one hundred years,

he decided to move to Beverly Hills, where the weather was much fairer! There he worked for the famous Scandia Restaurant and served the stars.

From Los Angeles he moved to Portland, where he worked with the Hilton Hotel. After a year and a half in Portland, Stig went to the island of Kauai, where he still chefed, but scuba diving became a new passion in his life. He left Kauai to attend scuba school in San Diego and became a certified scuba instructor. This was not a very lucrative living, so Stig headed back to Portland and worked at Nendel's for eight years.

It was while at Nendel's that Stig became highly involved in the Danish Brotherhood and the Danish community. He became a bit famous in the local chefs' cuisine market, and some of his cooking classes were televised. Stig started the Danish week at Nendel's, where he served Danish cuisine once a year for six years. This is also the time in Stig's life when family took on new meaning. He became the proud father to son, Nicolai and daughter Ashley. They were a delight in his life.

Utah was in his future now and opportunity arose with a young company named Flying J. Stig took on the tremendous task of elevating a chain of travel plaza interstate restaurants into a consistent, cost effective restaurant service unsurpassed by the transportation industry at that time. After an earlier divorce, Stig became intrigued with a rather independent woman, a single mother of three who worked for the same company. After falling in love, marriage was inevitable, and Stig was more than willing to take on the role of assisting in raising her three wonderful children, Nathan, Candace, and Will. The rest is history.

We celebrate each Christmas and most birthdays in the Danish tradition. We travel to Denmark every couple of years to reunite with Stig's loving family and to celebrate any occasion we can. It is Stig's greatest joy to be back in the Danish kitchen with his mother, who inspired and taught him, and with his father, too, preparing Danish cuisine. And oh, how the whole family loves to eat. For hours, I might add. Yes, eating in Denmark is an event. It is a time to socialize and enjoy the company of others—they call it *hygge*!

Stig and I now reside in Eden, Utah, with our dog Porter. Our grown children come to visit and ski in this resort community where the greatest powder on earth is truly an inspiration to hit the slopes! Stig currently works out of Texas for a chain of interstate travel plaza restaurants. But his heart is in the kitchen, and in his inspiration to create a legacy for his country and its great food and even greater people.

And now, *Cooking Danish* is his legacy to his family, his countrymen, and the rest of the world. May you learn to love cooking and eating Danish!

Susan Hansen
Wife of Chef Stig

Danish Flag
Dannebrog

Red and white, the national colors of Denmark, are drawn from the Danish flag. The Dannebrog is one of only three flags in the world with a name (the others are the Stars and Stripes of the United States and the Union Jack of Great Britain). According to popular legend, the Dannebrog "fell down from heaven" during the battle of Lyndanisse in Estonia on June 15, 1219. Led by Valdemar Sejrs on a Crusade to Estland, the army rallied and followed the heaven-sent banner to a resounding victory.

Danes revere the Dannebrog, and rightly so, as it is the oldest flag in the world in consecutive use without modification. They raise it across the country on special occasions and on ordinary days, as well. Its widespread use dates to a royal resolution of 1854 that declared it "permissible for everybody in the Royal Danish Kingdom to raise the Dannebrog flag on his own land."

Danes generally have an opinion about most things, but on this they all agree: The Dannebrog is the most handsome flag in the world.

The most northern lighthouse in Denmark, Skagen Lighthouse (Skagen's Fyrtårn) is on Jutland.

Conversion Chart and Assumptions
Ombytte tabel og formodning

All recipes are written using American measurements; should you want to use metric measurements, here are a few conversion charts for your use.

Weight and Volume
1 pound = 454 grams
1 ounce = 28 grams
1 cup = 2 dl
1 tablespoon = 15 ml
1 teaspoon = 5 ml

Butter
Margarine can generally be substituted when a recipe calls for butter.

Flour
Most baking recipes call for unbleached bread flour, but bleached bread flour can also be used.

Milk
Whenever milk is used in the recipes, you can generally choose between whole milk or 2% milk.

Temperature
If the oven is to be used for the recipe, it should be preheated to the given temperature before the dish is placed in the oven. All temperatures are given in Fahrenheit. If using Celsius, here are a few approximate temperature conversions for temperatures used in this book.

200° F = 95° C
225° F = 100° C
350° F = 175° C
375° F = 190° C
400° F = 200° C
425° F = 220° C
435° F = 225° C
450° F = 230° C
475° F = 245° C
500° F = 260° C

Note
Ingredients that are marked with an asterisk* indicate that a recipe for the ingredient may be found elsewhere in the book. Please refer to the index for the recipe.

Table of Contents

Sandwiches & Beverages

Smørrebrød & Drikkevarer

An Appetizing Introduction to Smørrebrød

With smørrebrød, Danish cuisine elevates the sandwich to a fine art. A hallmark of the Danish kitchen, the colorful appearance, appetizing blend of flavors, imaginative variety, and convenience of the Danish open-face sandwich—smørrebrød—give it international appeal.

Literally translated, smørrebrød means "bread and butter," but this is akin to describing a painting by Danish master Christian Kôbke as a piece of canvas with some color on it. Smørrebrød consists of a thin slice of dense bread evenly spread with creamy butter, finished off with an imaginative array of toppings artfully arranged to please both the eye and the palate.

Smørrebrød sandwiches offer convenience, variety, visual appeal, and taste satisfaction. They are the perfect complement to the contemporary emphasis on a healthy lifestyle and diet. Perhaps this is among the reasons why Denmark's contribution to worldwide cuisine is garnering interest and gaining popularity far beyond its borders.

How to Make Smørrebrød

There are no culinary secrets to making smørrebrød. You see all that goes in them at a glance, except the underlying slice of bread. Traditionally, you should never see the bread! Once you have learned to make just two or three kinds, with some of the dash and flair of the open-face sandwich—smørrebrød—you will be ready to tackle any number of varieties and create your own combinations. Most hungry smørrebrød makers would find sufficient supply in the refrigerator any day to make up at least two or three kinds. Don't be too ambitious when you begin. You can make a delightful meal with two or three well chosen varieties. Three or four smørrebrød should be sufficient for each person.

Five Easy Rules

Here are five five easy rules for successful smørrebrød making:

Bread

The bread should be fresh with a good crust. It should be close-textured to take the weight of the toppings. The use of white or pumpernickel bread is a matter of personal taste, but as a general rule it will be found that delicate flavors like mild cheeses, chicken and shrimp are best on white bread. Danish-style rye bread—pumpernickel—is an ideal base and is worth looking for, or bake a fresh loaf yourself. Cut pumpernickel into 1/4-inch slices; other breads may be sliced thicker. The slice should be about 2 x 4 inches, half of a slice from an ordinary sandwich loaf.

Toppings

Spread each slice with a good layer of butter, making sure the bread is completely covered. The butter on the bread provides a useful anchor for the toppings and stops any moisture going through to the bread to make it soggy. Generally speaking, one major ingredient—ham for example—is used for the topping, and should always be regarded as the most important part in terms of quantity. The toppings should be of ample proportions to cover the bread entirely. Meats and certain kinds of cheese can sometimes be folded or rolled to add height and often a piece of lettuce tucked under one corner gives the topping a lift.

Harbor of Skælskør on the island of Zealand—established in 1231, Skælskør is known as the sunshine city of Denmark.

Garnishing

Finally, the garnish adds a little crown of color and piquancy to each. Choose one that complements the flavor of the toppings and adds color as well. Aim for a fresh, simple effect rather than an overly ornamental or fussy arrangement. Garnishes range from a simple lettuce leaf, parsley sprig, radish roses, tomato and cucumber twists to delectable mayonnaises and salads. You will find they have quite a magical effect in highlighting the appeal of the simplest smørrebrød.

General Preparation

As in pastry or cake making, it helps to put out all the ingredients on the kitchen table before you begin—butter, bread, meats, cheeses, vegetables, etc. Hard-cook the eggs, and prepare scrambled eggs and meat jelly beforehand if they are to be used. Wash and dry lettuce, vegetables, or fruit to be eaten raw, and make any salads that may be used. Most people find it easier to do each of the four steps completely in turn, i.e. cut the bread into slices of the correct thickness and size, butter all bread, place all toppings on the bread, and finally add the garnishes.

Serving the Smørrebrød

Serve the finished smørrebrød on a flat dish or tray. Doilies can be used. A pie server or palette knife is useful for serving to individual plates. You need, of course, a knife and fork to eat the smørrebrød. A glass of cold Danish beer and an aquavit are excellent accompaniments to most all smørrebrød.

Danish Smorgasbord

Det store kolde bord

Here are two menus for Danish smorgasbords, or directly translated from Danish, "the big, cold table." The first lineup is a smaller presentation and the second one is a bit larger. Naturally you can delete items or add your own favorites as you please.

The smaller size!

Fish — Fisk

Pickled Herring with Onion — Spegesild med løg
Curried Herring* — Karrysild
Shrimp Salad* — Rejesalat
Dill-Cured Salmon* with Sauce — Graved Lax med sovs

Hot Dishes — Varme Retter

Danish Meatballs* with
Red Cabbage* and Pickled Green Tomatoes* —
Frikadeller med rødkål og syltede grønne tomater
Ground Beef Steak with
Grilled Onions and Pickled Squash* —
Hakkebøf med Løg og syltede græskar

Cheese — Ost

Havarti — Havarti
Danish Blue Cheese — Danish Blue
Smoked Buttermilk Cheese* — Knapost
Grapes and Radishes — Vindruer og Radisser

Cold Dishes — Kolde Retter

Chicken Liver Paté* with Pickled Cucumbers* —
Leverpostej med syltede asier
Thin Sliced Roast Beef with
Crisp Onions* and Remoulade* —
Tynd skåret Roastbeef med sprøde løg og remoulade

Dessert — Desert

Fruit Salad* — Frugtsalat

Breads — Brød

Pumpernickel* — Rugbrød
White Bread* — Franskbrød

Butter and Sandwich Spread* — Smør og Krydrefedt

Coffee and Assorted Cookies* —
Kaffe og udvalg af småkager

The larger size!

Fish — Fisk

Pickled Herring* with Onion — Spegesild med løg
Curried Herring* — Karrysild
Sherry Herring* — Sherrysild
Dill-Cured Salmon* with Sauce — Graved Lax med sovs
Mackerel in Tomato Sauce — Makrel in tomatsovs
Shrimp Salad* — Rejesalat
Deep Fried Fish Fillet with Remoulade* —
Friturestegt fiske filet med remoulade

Hot Dishes — Varme Retter

Danish Meatballs* with
Red Cabbage* and Pickled Green Tomatoes* —
Frikadeller med rødkål og syltede grønne tomater
Ground Beef Steak* with
Grilled Onions and Pickled Squash* —
Hakkebøf med stegte løg og syltede græskar
Fried Apples and Bacon* — Æbleflæsk
Danish Sausage* with Cucumber Salad* —
Medisterpølse med Agurkesalat

Cheese — Ost

Havarti — Havarti
Danish Blue Cheese — Danish Blue
Danish Brie* — Dansk Brie
Smoked Buttermilk Cheese* — Knapost
Grapes and Radishes — Vindruer og Radisser
Crackers — Kiks

Cold Dishes — Kolde Retter

Chicken Liver Paté* with Pickled Cucumbers* —
Leverpostej med syltede asier
Ham with Peas and Carrots Salad* —
Skinke med Italiensk salat
Sliced Salami with Onions and Meat Jelly* —
Spegepølse med løg og sky
Thin Sliced Roast Beef with
Crisp Onions* and Remoulade* —
Tynd skåret Roastbeef med sprøde løg og remoulade
Head Cheese with Pickled Red Beets* —
Sylte med syltede rødbeder
Sliced Boiled Potatoes, Eggs, and Tomatoes with Chives
— Skåret kogte kartofler, æg og tomater med purløg

Dessert — Desert

Fruit Salad* — Frugtsalat

Breads — Brød

Pumpernickel* — Rugbrød
Bolted Rye Bread* — Sigtebrød
White Bread* — Franskbrød

Butter & Sandwich Spread* — Smør og Krydrefedt

Coffee and Assorted Cookies* —
Kaffe og udvalg af småkager

Greenland Shrimp
Grønlandske Rejer

1/2 slice White Bread*
Butter
1 leaf butter lettuce
1 cup Greenland shrimp or similar
   bay shrimp
1 teaspoon mayonnaise
3 lemon twists
1 sprig dill weed

Shrimp Salad
Rejesalat

1/2 slice White Bread*
Butter
1 leaf butter lettuce
1/2 cup Shrimp Salad*
2 lemon twists
1 cucumber twist
2 asparagus spears
3 shrimp

Pickled Herring
Spegesild

1/2 slice Pumpernickel Bread*
Butter or Sandwich Spread*
1 leaf butter lettuce
6 pieces pickled herring
5 onion rings
1 tomato wedge

Curried Herring
Karrysild

1/2 slice Pumpernickel Bread*
Butter or Sandwich Spread*
1 leaf butter lettuce
1/2 cup Curried Herring*
3 slices hard-cooked egg
5 thin slices cucumber or
    1 tomato wedge

Sherry Herring
Sherrysild

1/2 slice Pumpernickel Bread*
Butter or Sandwich Spread*
1 leaf butter lettuce
4 or 5 pieces Sherry Herring*
1/2 tablespoon tomato and onion
    from Sherry Herring marinade
1 sprig parsley

Tomato Herring
Tomatsild

1/2 slice Pumpernickel Bread*
Butter or Sandwich Spread*
1 leaf butter lettuce
4 to 5 pieces Tomato Herring*
3 onion rings or 2 slices
    hard-cooked egg
2 tomato twists
1 sprig parsley

Cod Liver
Torske Lever

1/2 slice White Bread*
Butter
1 leaf butter lettuce
1 can cod liver (from Danish
   import store)
1 teaspoon mayonnaise
3 slices hard-cooked egg
2 pieces chives
1 sprig parsley

Mackerel in Tomato Sauce
Makrel i Tomat

1/2 slice White Bread*
Butter
1 leaf butter lettuce
1/2 can mackerel in tomato sauce
1/2 tablespoon mayonnaise
1 tablespoon chopped hard-
   cooked egg
2 lemon twists

Deep-Fried Fish Fillet
Friturestegt Fiskefilet

1/2 slice White Bread*
Butter
1 leaf butter lettuce
1 breaded fish fillet
1 teaspoon Remoulade*
5 small cooked shrimp
2 lemon twists
1 tomato twist
1 sprig parsley

Fish Patty
Fiskefrikadelle

1/2 slice White Bread*
Butter
1 leaf butter lettuce
1 Fish Patty,* sliced
1 teaspoon Remoulade*
3 lemon twists
1 sprig parsley

Sardines in Tomato Sauce
Sardiner i Tomat

1/2 slice Pumpernickel Bread*
Butter or Sandwich Spread*
1 leaf butter lettuce
1 (4-ounce) can sardines in
    tomato sauce
1 teaspoon mayonnaise
    (optional)
3 slices hard-cooked egg
    (optional)
3 lemon twists
1 sprig parsley

Cured Salmon
Graved Laks

1/2 slice White Bread*
Butter
1 leaf butter lettuce
6 slices Cured Salmon*
1 teaspoon Cured Salmon Sauce*
5 lemon twists
1 sprig dill weed

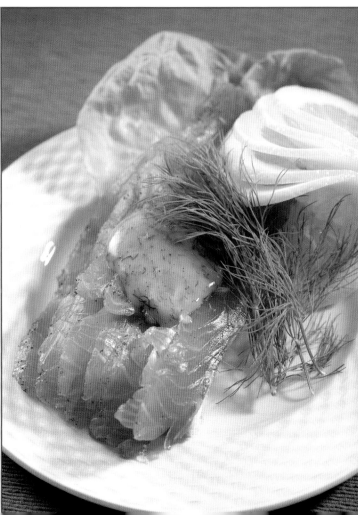

Roast Beef with Fried Egg
Roastbeef med Spejlæg

1/2 slice Pumpernickel Bread*
Butter or Sandwich Spread*
1 leaf butter lettuce
3 thin slices roast beef
   (not shaved)
1 fried egg
Freshly shredded horseradish
   to taste
3 thin slices cucumber
1 sprig parsley

Roast Beef
Roastbeef

1/2 slice Pumpernickel Bread*
Butter or Sandwich Spread*
1 leaf butter lettuce
3 thin slices roast beef
   (not shaved)
1 teaspoon Remoulade*
5 or 6 rings Crisp Onions*
2 orange twists
1 gherkin pickle, thinly sliced

Boiled Salted Meat
Saltkød

¹/₂ slice Pumpernickel Bread*
Butter or Sandwich Spread*
1 leaf butter lettuce
4 slices Boiled Salted Meat*
1 slice Meat Jelly*
3 thinly sliced sweet yellow
 onion rings
3 tomato twists

The "Veterinarian's" Midnight Snack
Dyrlægens Natmad

¹/₂ slice Pumpernickel Bread*
Butter or Sandwich Spread*
1 leaf butter lettuce
3 slices Chicken Liver Pâté*
2 slices Boiled Salted Meat*
1 slice Meat Jelly*
4 thinly sliced sweet yellow
 onion rings
1 thin tomato slice

Ham with Carrot & Pea Salad
Skinke med Italiensksalat

1/2 slice Pumpernickel Bread*
Butter or Sandwich Spread*
1 leaf butter lettuce
4 thin slices ham
1 tablespoon Carrot & Pea Salad*
2 asparagus spears
3 thin slices cucumber

Braised Pork Tenderloin
Brasered Svinemørbrad

1/2 slice Pumpernickel Bread*
Butter or Sandwich Spread*
1 leaf butter lettuce
6 slices Braised Pork Tenderloin*
6 to 8 slices mushrooms, sautéed
2 slices Pickled Red Beets*
1 sprig parsley

Pâté
Pate

¹/2 slice Pumpernickel Bread*
Butter or Sandwich Spread*
1 leaf butter lettuce
2 slices Dad's Pâté*
1 thin slice tomato
Pickled Cucumber*
1 sprig rosemary

Head Cheese
Sylte

¹/2 slice Pumpernickel Bread*
Butter or Sandwich Spread*
1 leaf butter lettuce
2 thick slices Mock Head Cheese*
2 slices Pickled Red Beets*
3 onion rings
1 teaspoon Mustard*

Salami
Spegepølse

1/2 slice Pumpernickel Bread*
Butter or Sandwich Spread*
1 leaf butter lettuce
4 slices large salami
   (do not slice too thin)
2 slices Meat Jelly*
Finely chopped sweet yellow
   onion
3 cucumber twists
2 tomato twists
1 sprig parsley

Pork "Sausage"
Rullepølse

1/2 slice Pumpernickel Bread*
Butter or Sandwich Spread*
1 leaf butter lettuce
5 slices Pork "Sausage"*
1 slice Meat Jelly*
2 thinly sliced sweet yellow
   onion rings
3 cucumber twists
1 thin slice tomato

Liver Pâté
Leverpostej

1/2 slice Pumpernickel Bread*
Butter or Sandwich Spread*
1 leaf butter lettuce
4 slices Chicken Liver Pâté*
1 slice bacon, crisp-cooked
2 slices Pickled Red Beets*
3 mushroom slices, sautéed
1 gherkin pickle, thinly sliced

H.C. Andersen's Favorite
H.C. Andersen's Favorit

1/2 slice Pumpernickel Bread*
Butter or Sandwich Spread*
1 leaf butter lettuce
3 slices Chicken Liver Pâté*
10 mushroom slices, sautéed
2 slices bacon, crisp-cooked
2 large slices tomato

Ground Beef Steak with Onions
Hakkebøf med løg

¹/2 slice Pumpernickel Bread
Butter or Sandwich Spread*
1 leaf butter lettuce
1 (4-ounce) Ground Beef Steak
    with Onions*
1 tablespoon Pickled Cucumber*
    or Cucumber Salad*
1 sprig parsley

Roast Leg of Lamb
Stegt Lammekølle

¹/2 slice Pumpernickel Bread*
Butter or Sandwich Spread*
1 leaf butter lettuce
3 thin slices Roast Leg of Lamb*
    (not shaved)
2 tablespoons Cucumber Salad*
3 tomato twists
1 sprig parsley

Breaded Pork Chop
Paneret Svinekotelet

¹/2 slice Pumpernickel Bread*
Butter or Sandwich Spread*
1 leaf butter lettuce
1 boneless Breaded Pork Chop*
2 tablespoons Red Cabbage*
3 orange twists
1 sprig parsley

The smørrebrød is thought to date back to medieval days when the gentry ate their meat served on rounds of bread rather than dinner plates. After the meal, this bread was given to the poor. Soaked with juices from the cooked meat, the bread was quite tasty. In the 1700s, the Danish upper class caught on to this and saved the bread for their own use. Single slices of bread topped with tasteful food combinations soon became a featured part of Danish cuisine. Smørrebrød was born, and it became widely popular.

Danish Sausage
Medisterpølse

1/2 slice Pumpernickel Bread*
Butter or Sandwich Spread*
1 leaf butter lettuce
2 pieces Danish Sausage,*
   cut into halves
1/4 cup Red Cabbage*
1 gherkin pickle, thinly sliced
2 orange twists

Fried Apples and Bacon
Æbleflæsk

1/2 slice Pumpernickel Bread*
Butter or Sandwich Spread*
1 leaf butter lettuce
1 serving Fried Apples and Bacon*
1 slice bacon, crisp-cooked
   and cut in half

Rotisserie Chicken
Grill Kylling

1/2 slice Pumpernickel Bread*
Butter
1 leaf butter lettuce
1 rotisserie-cooked chicken breast,
    all bones except the wing
    bone removed
2 tablespoons Cucumber Salad*
2 orange twists
Aluminum foil to cover the
    wing bone

Roast Duck
Andesteg

1/2 slice Pumpernickel Bread*
Butter or Sandwich Spread*
1 leaf butter lettuce
1 Roast Duck* breast, deboned
1/4 cup Red Cabbage*
3 prunes
2 orange twists

Danish Blue
Danish Blue

1/2 slice Pumpernickel Bread*
Butter or Sandwich Spread*
1 leaf butter lettuce
2 to 3 slices Danish Blue Cheese
3 walnut halves
1 bunch red or green grapes
3 orange twists

Smoked Buttermilk Cheese
Knapost

1/2 slice Pumpernickel Bread*
Butter or Sandwich Spread*
1 leaf butter lettuce
2 slices Smoked Buttermilk
    Cheese*
3 radishes
Chopped chives

Danish Blue with Egg Yolk
Danish Blue med Eggeblomme

1/2 slice Pumpernickel Bread*
Butter or Sandwich Spread*
2 to 3 slices Danish blue cheese
1 tomato slice
2 sweet onion rings
1 egg yolk
2 radishes
1 sprig parsley

Svenbo Cheese
Svenbo Ost

1/2 slice White Bread* or
    Pumpernickel Bread*
Butter
3 slices Svenbo cheese or
    Swiss cheese
1 strawberry, thinly sliced

Havarti Cheese
Havarti Ost

1/2 slice White Bread* or
    Pumpernickel Bread*
Butter
5 slices Havarti cheese
1 radish
1 bunch red or green grapes

By 1790, smørrebrød was prominently featured on the menu of Den Engelske Klub, a very exclusive Copenhagen club. The club prohibited smoking, dogs, the wearing of one's hat and above all, gaming—providing no incentive for inveterate gamblers, Danish or English, to top the smørrebrød with another slice of bread. This was probably a stroke of very good luck, for smørrebrød was allowed to evolve into a unique masterpiece of Danish cuisine, one favored by king, club member, and commoner alike.

Egg, Tomato and Cucumber
Æg, Tomat og Agurk

¹/₂ slice Pumpernickel Bread*
Butter or Sandwich Spread*
1 leaf butter lettuce
1 egg, hard-cooked and sliced
1 tomato, sliced
7 European cucumber slices
Chopped chives
Sprig of parsley

Egg Salad
Æggesalat

¹/₂ slice Pumpernickel Bread*
Butter or Sandwich Spread*
1 leaf butter lettuce
¹/₂ cup Egg Salad*
2 slices hard-cooked egg
4 slices radish

Fruit Salad
Frugtsalat

1/2 slice White Bread*
Butter
1 serving Fruit Salad*
2 orange twists
Shredded chocolate

Potato
Kartoffel

1/2 slice Pumpernickel Bread*
Butter or Sandwich Spread*
1 leaf butter lettuce
1 potato, boiled until fork tender
    and sliced
1/2 tablespoon Mustard*
3 slices tomato
1/4 teaspoon chopped chives

*My favorite sandwich as a child was pumpernickel bread with liver pâté. My mother would use double layer bread so it was easier to eat.
On special occasions we would get white bread with chocolate; this is a very thin sheet of chocolate on a slice of bread with butter. It tasted great, but was not the most nutritious sandwich.*

Peanut butter was not available in Denmark when I was a child. Today it is imported from the USA and only sold in specialty shops, and the price shows!

Roasted Chicken Leg
Grilled Kyllingelår

1/2 slice Pumpernickel Bread*
Butter
1 roasted chicken leg
3 cucumber twists
1 paper frill to put over leg bone

Chocolate
Chokolade

1/2 slice White Bread*
Butter
6 thin slices chocolate from
      Danish import store
3 orange wedges

Sandwich Toppings

Traditionally built upon a thin dense slice of bread, toppings are as varied as the chef's imagination and the diner's preference. An endless variety of meats, seafood, cheeses, eggs, fresh vegetables, salads and colorful condiments may be used in making smørrebrød. Many Danish hotels and restaurants offer their own special combinations. Since the beginning of the last century, the famous Copenhagen restaurant Ida Davidsen's has offered patrons a list of smørrebrød toppings some three feet long.

Shrimp Salad
Rejesalat

Serves 4

1 cup fresh or frozen small
    bay shrimp
1/2 cup (3/8-inch slices) fresh or
    drained canned asparagus
1/2 cup mayonnaise
1/8 teaspoon salt
Pinch of ground white pepper
Cooked macaroni (optional)
White Bread*

This is traditionally made with white asparagus, which is in every market in Denmark, but can be hard to find outside of Europe. Green asparagus works fine and actually adds a little color to the salad.

1 Place frozen shrimp in a strainer and thaw under cold running water for several minutes. Remove a few at a time and squeeze gently to remove excess water. Cook fresh asparagus in water in a saucepan for several minutes. Drain and rinse with cold water to cool; drain again.

2 Combine the mayonnaise, salt and white pepper in a medium bowl and mix well. Reserve a small amount of the asparagus and shrimp for garnish. Add the remaining shrimp and asparagus and mix gently. Mix in the macaroni, if desired. Chill, covered, in the refrigerator for several hours. Spoon into a serving bowl and serve with fresh White Bread.

Herring

Sild

A Danish Favorite!

You would be hard-pressed to find a Danish spread that doesn't include herring. This favorite fish has figured prominently in the Danish diet for generations and is prepared in a great variety of ways. The most popular preparations are smoked herring and pickled herring. The pickled herring actually starts out as a salted herring that is prepared during the autumn season and is later rinsed and pickled.

Stories dating back to the early 1200s describe herring as silver in the water. There were so many of them in the Strait of Øresund that one could scoop them out of the water with a net. In 1300, more than 20,000 people gathered on the coast of Øresund in September and early October for the herring run. By 1600, the herring were not as numerous; the demand for herring also had fallen with the rise of family farms.

I remember catching herring as a boy when they traveled past a bridge in town; I simply lowered a fishing line with four or five hooks attached. When schools of herring swam by I pulled the line up and would catch two or three at a time by hooking them in the side. On those days there was fresh fried herring for dinner!

Curried Herring
Karrysild

Serves 6 to 8

2 teaspoons heavy cream or milk
1 tablespoon curry powder
1 cup mayonnaise
1 Granny Smith apple or pear,
    peeled and chopped into
      1/4-inch cubes
1 1/2 cups (1/2-inch slices)
    pickled herring
3 eggs, hard-cooked for
    12 minutes and diced with
    an egg slicer
Pumpkernickel Bread*

Do not use pickled herring in sour cream for this recipe.

1 Combine the cream and curry powder in a bowl and mix well. Stir in the mayonnaise. Add the apple, herring and eggs and mix gently.

2 Marinate, covered, in the refrigerator for at least 2 hours or up to 2 weeks. Serve on Pumpernickel Bread with an aquavit! Skål!

Sherry Herring
Sherrysild

Serves 4 to 6

1 Roma tomato
1 tablespoon minced onion
1 tablespoon ketchup
1/2 teaspoon red wine vinegar
1/3 cup dry sherry
1 teaspoon sugar
1/8 teaspoon thyme
1/8 teaspoon ground pepper
1 cup (1-inch pieces)
    pickled herring
Hard-cooked eggs, sliced
Tomato twist
Pumpernickel Bread*

For a milder flavor, use the onions that usually come in the jar with the herring. Do not use pickled herring in sour cream for this recipe.

1 Cut the tomato into halves and discard the seeds; cut into 1/4-inch pieces. Combine the tomato with the onion, ketchup, vinegar, sherry, sugar, thyme and ground pepper in a medium bowl and mix well.

2 Add the herring and mix gently. Marinate, covered, in the refrigerator for at least 8 hours or up to 3 weeks. Spoon into a serving bowl and top with hard-cooked eggs and a tomato twist. Serve with Pumpernickel Bread.

Tomato Herring
Tomatsild

Serves 4

1 Roma tomato
1/4 cup dehydrated minced onion
1/2 teaspoon chopped fresh chive
1/2 tablespoon olive oil
1 teaspoon red wine vinegar
1/3 cup ketchup
1/3 tablespoon dry sherry
1/8 teaspoon ground pepper
1 cup (1-inch pieces)
    pickled herring
Hard-cooked eggs, sliced
Tomato twist
Pumpernickel Bread*

Do not use pickled herring in sour cream for this recipe.

1 Cut the tomato into halves and discard the seeds; cut into 1/4-inch pieces. Combine the tomato with the onion, chive, olive oil, vinegar, ketchup, sherry and pepper in a bowl and mix well.

2 Add the herring and mix gently. Marinate, covered, in the refrigerator for at least 8 hours or up to 2 weeks. Spoon into a serving bowl and top with hard-cooked eggs and a tomato twist. Serve with Pumpkernickel Bread and a cold beer.

Herring Salad
Sildesalat

Serves 4 to 6

3 tablespoons juice from pickled
    red beets
1/2 cup sour cream
1 teaspoon grated horseradish
1/2 teaspoon ground pepper
1 cup (1-inch pieces) pickled
    herring
1 cup (1/4-inch cubes) cooked and
    peeled white potato
1 Granny Smith apple, peeled and
    cut into 1/4-inch cubes
1 cup (1/4-inch cubes) Pickled
    Red Beets*
1 cup (1/4-inch cubes)
    Pickled Cucumber*
2 eggs, hard-cooked for 12 minutes
    and cut into quarters
Parsley
Pumpkernickel Bread*

1 Combine the pickled beet juice with the sour cream, horseradish and pepper in a large bowl. Add the herring, potato, apple, beets and cucumber and mix gently.

2 Spoon into a serving bowl and top with the egg quarters and parsley. Serve on or with fresh Pumpkernickel Bread.

Dill-Cured Salmon with Sauce
Gravad laks med sovs

Serves 6 to 8

The dill weed used to cure the salmon can be used in the sauce.
If the sauce should separate, start over with a small amount of mustard
and add the separated sauce gradually, mixing until smooth.

Salmon

1/3 cup sugar

1/3 cup kosher salt

1 tablespoon ground pepper

1 (2-pound) very fresh
   salmon fillet

1 tablespoon aquavit (optional)

1 to 2 bunches fresh dill weed

Sauce

2 tablespoons Mustard*

1 tablespoon sugar

2 tablespoons red wine vinegar

1/2 cup olive oil or vegetable oil

2 tablespoons finely chopped
   fresh dill weed

Salmon

1 Mix the sugar, kosher salt and pepper together. Sprinkle some of the mixture into a deep glass dish. Cut the salmon into halves, discarding all bones. Place one piece of the salmon in the dish and sprinkle with aquavit. Sprinkle generously with the seasoning mixture and top with a generous amount of the dill weed.

2 Sprinkle the remaining piece of salmon with the seasoning mixture. Place on top of the dill weed and sprinkle with the remaining seasoning mixture. Top with a plate or lid and a 4- to 5-pound weight.

3 Marinate in the refrigerator for 24 to 36 hours, turning two or three times each day. Remove the salmon from the refrigerator and scrape clean. Cut into very thin slices.

Sauce

Combine the Mustard and sugar in a bowl and mix well. Beat in the vinegar and then the oil gradually. Add the dill weed and mix until the consistency of mayonnaise. Spread over the salmon on your favorite bread. Serve with beer and aquavit.

Cold Smoked Salmon Lox
Røget laks

Makes 1 pound

1/2 cup salt
1/2 cup packed brown sugar
2 cups cold water
1 (1-pound) fresh salmon fillet, boned
4 ounces small hickory wood pieces
Pumpernickel Bread* or White Bread*

1 Mix the salt and brown sugar in an 8×8-inch glass dish. Add the water and mix until the salt and brown sugar dissolve completely. Rinse the salmon in cold water and pat dry. Add to the dish, immersing completely. Marinate, covered, in the refrigerator for 8 hours.

2 Remove the salmon from the brine mixture and pat dry; do not rinse. Discard the brine, rinse the dish and return the salmon to the dish. Cover with plastic wrap and chill in the refrigerator for 24 hours.

3 Place the salmon on the top rack of an electric smoker grill; place a cold-smoke heat barrier on the lower rack and place a pan of ice on the heat barrier. Load the wood in the smoker compartment.

4 Smoke the salmon at 225 degrees for 20 minutes. Turn off the heat and let stand in the smoker for 1 hour. Repeat the process of heating at 225 for 20 minutes and holding for 1 hour. Test the salmon for smoke flavor, which may vary with the outside temperature. Remove the skin if the salmon was smoked with the skin.

5 Chill the salmon in the refrigerator for several hours. Cut into thin slices and serve on Pumpernickel Bread or White Bread with a cold beer.

Smoked Salmon Salad
Røget laksesalat

Serves 4

12 fresh or drained canned asparagus spears
1/2 cup mayonnaise
1/2 teaspoon granulated onion
1/2 teaspoon granulated garlic
1/2 teaspoon salt
1/2 teaspoon ground pepper
4 eggs, hard-cooked for 12 minutes and cut into cubes with an egg slicer, cutting twice
1 cup (1/4-inch cubes) Smoked Salmon*

1 Cut the asparagus into 1/2-inch pieces. Steam or boil fresh asparagus in water in a saucepan for 3 to 4 minutes; drain. Rinse with cold water and drain again.

2 Combine the mayonnaise, onion, garlic, salt and pepper in a bowl and mix well. Reserve a small amount of the asparagus and eggs for garnish and add the remaining asparagus and eggs to the mayonnaise mixture. Stir in the salmon.

3 Spoon into a serving dish and top with the reserved asparagus and eggs. Serve on fresh baked bread or on crackers as a snack.

Boiled Salted Meat
Saltkød

Makes 2 pounds

2 pounds beef eye of round
1/2 recipe Salt Brine* (below)

1 Trim any silver from the beef. Combine the beef with the Salt Brine in a glass dish. Let stand in the brine for 8 days, turning daily. Remove the beef and discard the brine.

2 Bring enough fresh water to cover the beef to a boil in a saucepan. Add the beef and return to a boil. Reduce the heat and simmer for 1 hour. Turn off the heat and let the beef stand in the water for 1 hour longer.

3 Remove the beef to a refrigerator-safe container and add enough of the cooking liquid to cover the beef. Chill in the refrigerator until cold. Slice very thin for smørrebrød topping.

Salt Brine
Saltlage

Makes 4 quarts

1 gallon water
3 1/2 cups kosher salt
1/3 cup sugar
5 bay leaves
1/4 cup dried juniper berries
1 tablespoon peppercorns

Combine the water with the kosher salt, sugar, bay leaves, juniper berries and peppercorns in a stainless steel or other noncorrosive saucepan. Bring to a boil and boil for 2 to 3 minutes. Cool in the pan and chill in the refrigerator for 8 hours or longer. Use the brine for Boiled Salted Meat*, Rullepølse* or other dishes.

Dine onboard the Ferries – Spise ombord på Færgerne
When traveling in Denmark it has been a tradition for years to eat on board the ferry when going from one island to another. The restaurant on board serves Open-Face Sandwiches and hot dishes; they are served quickly for the short ferry ride.

As a teenager, I worked on one of these ferries sailing from Nyborg to Korsør. It was interesting work. You worked really hard to get the food out to the guests who were in a hurry to get the food for the 55-minute ferry ride; then you cleaned up and waited for the next departure.

However, with all the new bridges being built this tradition is slowly disappearing.

Pork "Sausage"
Rullepølse

Serves 12 to 15

1 rack pork spareribs
1/2 ounce unflavored gelatin
1 teaspoon granulated onion
1 teaspoon ground allspice
1/2 tablespoon ground pepper
1/2 bunch fresh parsley
1 recipe Salt Brine*

There are special presses for this in Denmark, but a heavy weight works well. The recipe can be made with breast of veal or lamb, but the pork spareribs are readily available and don't have too much fat.

1 Remove the bones from the pork by cutting down the middle of each bone, scraping the meat off the tops of the bones and pulling out the bones. Cut out the cartilage that leads to each bone and the bone on the top of the meat. Trim the pork into a rectangular piece, reserving the trimmings.

2 Place the trimmings on the pork and roll it up to enclose the trimmings, taking care that it is the same thickness throughout. Trim the ends. Unroll the pork and sprinkle with the gelatin, onion, allspice and pepper. Layer the parsley leaves over the pork and roll again as tightly as possible; tie with butcher's twine.

3 Place the roll in a plastic container and cover with the Salt Brine. Place a plate on the top to keep the roll submerged and cover. Chill in the refrigerator for 5 days, turning the roll every day. Remove the roll from the brine and pat dry with paper towels.

4 Add enough fresh water to cover the roll to a very large saucepan. Bring to a boil and add the pork roll. Return to a boil and reduce the heat. Simmer for 1 hour. Turn off the heat and let the roll stand in the water for 1 hour longer.

5 Remove the roll from the water and place in a pan. Place a second pan on top of the roll and place a 30-pound weight in the pan. Chill in the refrigerator for 8 hours or longer. Remove the twine and slice very thin for smørrebrød topping.

Dad's Pâté

Far's pate

Serves 10 to 12

2 pounds ground unseasoned
    fresh pork
1 1/2 tablespoons dehydrated
    chopped onion
1 1/2 teaspoons chopped
    fresh garlic
1 teaspoon ground rosemary
1 teaspoon ground marjoram
1/2 teaspoon dried thyme leaves
1 teaspoon salt
1 teaspoon ground pepper
2 eggs
1 cup heavy cream
1/2 cup red wine
1 cup (1/4-inch cubes) ham
8 ounces chicken livers,
    coarsely chopped
10 to 14 slices bacon
2 bay leaves
1 sprig fresh rosemary

1 Combine the ground pork, onion, garlic, rosemary, marjoram, thyme, salt and pepper in a mixing bowl and mix well. Mix in the eggs one at a time. Add the cream and then the wine gradually, mixing well after each addition. Stir in the ham and liver.

2 Line an 8×8-inch glass baking dish with the bacon, covering the bottom and sides well and reserving some for the top. Spoon the meat mixture into the prepared dish and cover with the remaining bacon. Top with the bay leaves and rosemary sprig. Place in a larger pan with 1/2 inch water.

3 Bake at 350 degrees for 2 hours or to 180 degrees on a meat thermometer. Cool in the dish on a wire rack. Chill in the refrigerator for 8 hours or longer.

4 Remove any excess fat and place on a serving plate. Cut into thin slices and serve on fresh Pumpkernickel Bread* with Pickled Cucumber* and Red Beets*. Enjoy with a cold beer.

Chicken Liver Pâté

Leverpostej

Serves 30 to 32

3/4 cup (1 1/2 sticks) butter
1 1/4 cups all-purpose flour
8 cups (1/2 gallon) 2% milk
1/4 cup dehydrated chopped onions
6 tablespoons sugar
1/4 cup salt
2 teaspoons ground white pepper
4 pounds chicken livers
4 pounds pork fat
8 eggs

This makes a lot, but it can be prepared in several loaf pans, frozen and thawed before baking. Do not freeze baked pâté, as it will crumble when thawed.

1 Melt the butter in a heavy medium saucepan over medium heat. Add the flour and cook for 1 minute, stirring constantly. Add the milk and bring to a boil, stirring constantly. Stir in the onions, sugar, salt and white pepper. Boil for several minutes, watching carefully to avoid burning. Cool the mixture and chill in the refrigerator for 8 hours.

2 Grind the livers and pork fat in a meat grinder. Grind just the fat or both the fat and livers again. Remove the chilled mixture from the refrigerator and mix in the eggs. Add the ground liver and pork fat and mix well.

3 Pack the mixture into eight 4×8-inch loaf pans or sixteen 3×5-inch pans. Place the pans in larger pans and add enough water to reach halfway up the sides. Bake the larger loaf pans at 350 degrees for 2 to 2 1/2 hours and the smaller pans for 1 3/4 to 2 hours. Cool the pâté completely before serving. Serve on Pumpernickel Bread* with Red Beets*.

Smoker for Cheese
Osterygeovn

1 (16×16-inch) red brick
2 (8×16-inch) red bricks
4 (4×8-inch) red bricks
1 heat duct piece
Dry straw

1 Place the 16×16-inch brick on a flat area that does not present a fire hazard. Close any windows nearby to avoid smoke in the house. Build a rectangular box to fit the heat duct with the remaining bricks (see the photographs).

2 Place the straw in the smoker and light the straw to create a good fire. Place the heat duct over the rectangle to act as a chimney. Place the cheese to be smoked in a heatproof strainer in the chimney. Place a lid on the chimney and smoke with strong smoke for 1 to 1½ minutes.

Smoked Buttermilk Cheese
Knapost

Makes 1 cheese

8 cups (1/2 gallon) cultured
    low-fat buttermilk
1/4 cup heavy cream
1/2 teaspoon caraway seeds
1/4 teaspoon salt
1/8 teaspoon white pepper
1 teaspoon caraway seeds
3 handfuls straw

1 Place the buttermilk in a heavy saucepan and cover. Place over the lowest possible heat and heat without stirring for 11/2 hours. The buttermilk should separate into a thick cream on top of watery whey. Skim off the cream and place in a strainer lined with cheesecloth; let drain for several minutes. Place over a bowl and drain in the refrigerator for up to 8 hours or longer.

2 Combine the chilled cream with the heavy cream, 1/2 teaspoon caraway seeds, the salt and white pepper; mix well. Serve the cheese fresh or proceed with smoking.

3 Place a cheesecloth on a work surface and sprinkle with 1 teaspoon caraway seeds. Place the cheese on the seeds and lift in the cheesecloth into a strainer, pressing lightly into the shape of the strainer.

4 Invert the cheese onto a plate, remove the cheesecloth and return the cheese to the strainer. Prepare the Smoker for Cheese* with the straw. Smoke the cheese according to the smoker directions for 11/2 minutes. Serve the cheese with Pumpernickel Bread*, radishes, salt and pepper. Unused cheese may be stored in the refrigerator for several days.

Smoked Country Cheese

Smoked Country Cheese, or Rygeost fra Fyn, is very similar to the Smoked Buttermilk Cheese and takes a little longer, but it is creamier and has less of the buttermilk taste. It is very popular on the island of Fyn. In the summer, they smoke the cheese right in the farmers' market. It is made using 3 cups of buttermilk and 9 cups of whole milk. The mixture is heated without stirring over the lowest possible heat for 41/2 to 5 hours. At that point the recipe is prepared exactly like the Smoked Buttermilk Cheese.

Egg Salad
Æggesalat

Serves 4

9 eggs, chilled
3/4 cup mayonnaise
1 tablespoon Mustard*
1/4 tablespoon granulated onion
1/4 tablespoon granulated garlic
1/2 teaspoon salt
1/2 teaspoon ground
    white pepper

Adding cold eggs to boiling water will help prevent their cracking. It is generally easier to peel eggs that are several days old than eggs that are fresh.

1 Bring a saucepan of water to a boil and add the cold eggs. Reduce the heat and simmer for 12 minutes. Cool the eggs under cold water and peel. Dice the eggs by cutting twice with an egg slicer.

2 Combine the mayonnaise, Mustard, onion, garlic, salt and white pepper in a bowl and mix well. Fold in the eggs. Chill, covered, in the refrigerator for several hours. Serve on fresh White Bread* or on Pumpernickel Bread* as a smørrebrød.

Carrot and Pea Salad
Italiensksalat

Makes 2 1/4 cups

1 cup (1/4-inch cubes)
    peeled carrots
1 cup frozen green peas
1/4 cup mayonnaise
Pinch of salt
1/8 teaspoon ground white pepper
Fresh green or white asparagus,
    cooked and drained

1 Bring enough water to cover the carrots to a boil in a small saucepan. Add the carrots and boil for 5 to 6 minutes. Add the frozen peas and return to a boil. Drain the vegetables in a strainer. Rinse under cold water and let stand until cool.

2 Combine the mayonnaise, salt and white pepper in a bowl and mix well. Add the carrots and peas and mix gently. Chill in the refrigerator for several hours. Serve on ham for a smørrebrød and top with asparagus.

Fruit Salad
Frugtsalat

Serves 4

1 (15-ounce) can fruit cocktail
1 cup heavy whipping cream,
   whipped
Grated chocolate
3 orange slice twists
1 maraschino cherry

1 Drain the fruit cocktail in a small strainer for 30 minutes, discarding the juice. Combine the fruit with the whipped cream in a small bowl and mix well.

2 Spoon into a serving bowl and top with grated chocolate, orange twists and a maraschino cherry. Serve as a salad or as a topping for a smørrebrød on White Bread*.

Scrambled Egg Garnish
Æggestand

Serves 6 to 8

4 eggs
1/2 cup heavy cream or
   half-and-half
1/2 teaspoon salt
1/4 teaspoon ground white pepper
1 tablespoon butter
Finely chopped chives

1 Combine the eggs with the cream, salt and white pepper in a small bowl and whip until well mixed. Melt the butter in a small nonstick skillet over medium heat; do not allow to brown.

2 Add the eggs to the skillet and cook over medium heat just until set, stirring and scraping the bottom of the skillet with a spatula; do not overcook. Spoon into a 5-inch strainer, pressing with the spatula until packed.

3 Chill in the refrigerator for several hours. Invert onto a serving plate and sprinkle with chives. Serve as a garnish for Smoked Salmon* or trout.

Crisp Onions
Sprøde løg

Serves 4

1 yellow onion
1 cup buttermilk
2 cups (about) all-purpose flour
Vegetable oil for deep-frying

1 Slice the onion as thinly as possible. Combine with the buttermilk in a medium bowl, stirring gently to separate the slices into rings. Let stand for 8 minutes or longer. Drain and discard the buttermilk.

2 Place the flour in a plastic bag. Add the onion rings a few at a time, coating well. Shake off any excess flour.

3 Deep-fry in heated vegetable oil for 3 minutes and remove to paper towels to drain. Repeat the process with the remaining onion rings. Serve as a garnish or as a snack.

Meat Jelly
Sky

Makes 1 cup

$1/2$ cup water
1 ($1/4$-ounce) envelope
    unflavored gelatin
1 teaspoon beef base or crushed
    bouillon cube
$1/2$ tablespoon dry sherry
$1/2$ cup cold water

1 Bring $1/2$ cup water to a boil in a small saucepan. Add the gelatin and beef base, stirring to dissolve completely. Return to a boil and remove from the heat. Stir in the sherry and $1/2$ cup cold water.

2 Pour the mixture into a square $11/2$- to 2-cup dish. Chill in the refrigerator until firm. Dip the bowl in hot water for several seconds to loosen the jelly and invert it onto a plate.

3 Cut the jelly into strips to use as a garnish for smørrebrød.

Sandwich Spread
Krydrefedt

Makes 2¹/₂ cups

1 Granny Smith apple
2 cups melted fat
1 small yellow onion,
    finely chopped
1 teaspoon dried thyme leaves
¹/₂ teaspoon ground pepper

The fat from a roasted duck has a great flavor and can be used in this recipe, but it should be mixed with pork fat, as it melts at room temperature.

1 Peel and finely chop the apple, discarding the seeds. Combine the apple with the fat in a small saucepan and add the onion, thyme and pepper. Simmer for 20 minutes.

2 Spoon into a small bowl and chill in the refrigerator until firm. Use as a substitute for butter on Pumpernickel Bread* for smørrebrød.

Remoulade
Remoulade

Makes 1 cup

¹/₂ cup mayonnaise
¹/₂ cup hot dog relish
¹/₄ teaspoon Mustard*
1 teaspoon sugar

Be sure to use real mayonnaise in this recipe rather than a salad dressing product.

Combine the mayonnaise, relish, Mustard and sugar in a medium bowl and mix well. Chill in the refrigerator for several hours to blend the flavors. Serve on smørrebrød.

Tivoli – Tivoli
The world famous Tivoli Gardens in Copenhagen is a great place for dining, fun, and entertainment.

Tivoli was established in 1843 by Georg Carsensen with permission from King Christian VIII for a five-year permit to operate an entertainment park. This gorgeous spot in Copenhagen has been developed for more than 150 years to be an international attraction and a must-visit spot in Denmark.

With a great variety of restaurants, Tivoli is a great place to visit just to dine. But of course it offers so much more, with rides and world-renowned entertainers.

Serving Aquavit
Serverer Snaps

Aquavit is a Scandinavian distilled beverage of about 40 percent alcohol by volume, generally flavored with caraway seeds and other herbs. Its name comes from the Latin aqua vitae, "water of life." The earliest known reference to aquavit is in a letter written by the Danish lord of Bergenshus Castle in 1531. In the years since, a number of traditions have grown up around this favored liquor.

Served ice cold, aquavit is often presented in a stemmed shot glass. The stem on the glass prevents one's hand from warming the contents. While many people drink a full shot at once, I prefer to savor its aromas and flavors. I make a shot last as long as two or three sips.

Ertholmene, the Harbor of Christiansø, built in 1684 by King Christian V.

No matter how you drink it, the prescribed toast to offer with a glass of aquavit is skål—cheers! According to the folks at Carlsberg Breweries, the toast skål refers to the skol or drinking bowl made from the actual skull of one's enemy killed in battle. The message: Don't mess with the Danes!

Aquavit is the perfect accompaniment to open-face sandwiches, smorgasbord and such hot dishes as Yellow Split Pea Soup (page 113). Some people like a shot of aquavit first thing in the morning to kick start their day!

To enjoy aquavit at its best, serve it ice cold. Store it in the freezer as this high-proof alcohol will not freeze. Here's how to keep it chilled as you serve it:

- Place the bottle of aquavit in a large juice can. Fill the can with water.
- Place it in the freezer overnight.
- Once the water has frozen solid, remove from the freezer and run hot water over the can.
- When it loosens, pull the bottle and ice from the can. This will keep the aquavit cold while serving.
- Set the ice-wrapped bottle in a bowl or shallow container. Keep an eye on the melting water!

Danish Mary
Dansk Mary

Serves 1

1/4 cup (2 ounces) aquavit
3/4 cup (6 ounces) tomato juice or
   Bloody Mary mix
Pinch of ground pepper
5 ice cubes
1 lemon wedge
1 green onion with top

Combine the aquavit, tomato juice and pepper with the ice in a glass and stir to mix well. Make a slit between the peel and the flesh of the lemon wedge and place on the rim of the glass. Cut the top of the green onion into a tassel and add to the glass.

The Hamlet
Hamlet

Serves 1

3 tablespoons (1 1/2 ounces)
   Peter Heering (cherry liqueur)
3 tablespoons (1 1/2 ounces)
   aquavit

Combine the Peter Heering and aquavit in a cocktail shaker and shake well. Strain into a martini glass.

Tivoli Special
Tivoli special

Serves 1

2 tablespoons (1 ounce) aquavit
1 teaspoon fresh lemon juice
5 ice cubes
Ginger ale
1 lemon wedge

Combine the aquavit with the lemon juice and ice cubes in a glass and stir to mix well. Add enough ginger ale to fill the glass. Make a slit between the peel and the flesh of the lemon wedge and place on the rim of the glass.

Danish Beer

Dansk Øl

Danes love their beer, and it occupies an important place at the Danish table. In recent years the number of local breweries in Denmark has multiplied, resulting in finely crafted beer for almost every taste. Favorites both at home and abroad include brews produced by the internationally famous Carlsberg Brewery which is, among the largest in the world.

Beer drinking has deep roots in Denmark. Early evidence of a beer-like beverage was unearthed in the town of Egtved on Jutland. In a burial mound dating back 3,450 years to the Bronze Age, archeologists found the body of a young girl, 16–18 years old when she died. She was wrapped in cow hide and a woolen blanket. Next to her lay a birch bark bowl that contained a fermented fruit beverage.

The Vikings, those globe-trotting Danish adventurers of the 700s through the 1100s, were known for their beer-like beverage mjød or "mead" made with honey, berries, and herbs. As farming developed, grains became part of the brewing process.

Beer became the beverage of choice in the 1500s, as clean drinking water was often unavailable in many parts of the country. Its growing popularity did not escape the crown's notice. The king began taxing beer sales. Dark ales and weak table beers were the favorites.

By the mid-1800s, clear golden lagers were all the rage in Denmark and across Europe. Brewers scrambled to meet the demand. The country's three largest breweries were founded: Carlsberg, Ceres, and Tuborg. In 1883, a young Danish scientist working for Carlsberg developed the first pure strain of beer yeast, and in the process revolutionized the brewing of lager and ale the world over. As the big breweries flourished, small town brewers closed their doors. However, in recent years microbreweries have seen a resurgence in popularity as Danes once again seek out handcrafted, quality beers.

Exported worldwide, Danish beer is available in most locales. I include a couple of my own recipes for home brewers. Inspired by Carlsberg's, Albani's and Harboe's labels for their respective Elephant, Giraffe and Polar Bear beers, I named two of my own brews after animals: Lazy Moose (for the creature that took a nap in our backyard) and Porter—Man's Best Friend (after our dog). In 2005, at a national competition in Baltimore, the Lazy Moose was awarded a silver medal in the dark lager category.

Lazy Moose Golden Lager

Makes 10 gallons

14 pounds 2-row German
    pilsner malt
1 pound cracked Munich malt
1 1/2 pounds cracked Cara-Pils Malt
1 pound cracked Cara-Vienne Malt
1 pound cracked torrified wheat
6 gallons (130-degree) water

1. Grains should be at about 60 degrees. Add the grains to 6 gallons water in a brew pot and mix well. The mixture should stabilize at 122 degrees.
2. Heat to 132 degrees. Cover and hold for 30 minutes, stirring gently every 5 minutes.

1 gallon (175-degree) water

1. Add 1 gallon water to the mash and heat quickly to 148 degrees. Hold for 45 minutes. Raise the heat to 155 degrees and hold for 15 minutes.
2. Test with iodine to get a red-brown color; continue steeping for up to 20 minutes longer if necessary.

2 ounces black malt, finely crushed
1/2 gallon (170-degree) water

Mix the black malt with 1/2 gallon water and add to the mash. Mash out at 165 degrees.

10 gallons (175-degree) water

Sparge gradually with the water. Drain the wort slowly into the brew pot and bring to a boil. Stop the run-off when the gravity falls below 1.008 or when the pH is greater than 6.0 to 6.1.

1/2 ounce Willamette Leaf Hops,
    Alpha 4.5%
1 ounce Fuggle Leaf Hops,
    Alpha 4.0%

Add the boiling hops and keep at a rolling boil, loosely covered, for 35 minutes.

1 teaspoon Irish moss

Add the Irish moss and boil, loosely covered, for 30 minutes.

2 ounces wild hops picked at
    Pineview Lake, Utah, or
    Czech Saaz Hops
1 ounce Czech Saaz Leaf Hops,
    Alpha 3.5%

1. Turn off the heat and add the hops for aroma; let steep for 15 minutes. Cool to 70 to 75 degrees and add to two 6 1/2-gallon carboys. Aerate with straight oxygen for 50 seconds
2. Pitch yeast starter made from Pilsner Lager Yeast. Leave at 70 to 75 degrees overnight. Store at 50 degrees for 2 weeks.
3. Rack into two 5-gallon secondary fermenters and ferment for 2 to 3 weeks at 38 to 40 degrees.

3/4 cup corn sugar and 2 cups
    water to prime each carboy
    for bottling

Original specific gravity: 1.056   Alcohol: 7.5%
Terminal specific gravity: 1.020   Alcohol: 2.8%
Final specific gravity: 1.010   Alcohol: 1.2%
Final alcohol: 6.3%

Porter: Man's Best Friend

Makes 10 gallons

18 pounds cracked 2-row malt

1 pound cracked 55L British Crystal Malt

12 ounces cracked brown malt

10 ounces cracked American Chocolate Malt

1 pound cracked torrified wheat

6 1/2 gallons (130-degree) water

1. Grains should be at 60 degrees. Add the grains to 6 1/2 gallons water in a brew pot and mix well. It should stabilize at 122 degrees.

2. Heat to 132 degrees and cover. Hold for 30 minutes, stirring gently every 5 minutes.

1 gallon (175-degree) water

1. Add 1 gallon water and heat quickly to 148 degrees. Hold for 45 minutes.

2. Raise the heat to 155 degrees and hold for 15 minutes. Test with iodine to get a red-brown color; continue steeping for up to 20 minutes longer if necessary.

3. Mash out at 160 degrees.

10 gallons (170-degree) water

Sparge slowly with 10 gallons water, then gradually drain the wort into the brew pot. Bring to a boil. Stop the run-off when the specific gravity falls below 1.008 or the pH is greater than 6.0 to 6.1.

3 ounces East Kent Goldings Hops, pellets, Alpha: 5.9%

Add the boiling hops and keep at a rolling boil, loosely covered, for 35 minutes.

1 teaspoon Irish moss

Add the Irish moss and boil for 30 minutes.

1 ounce Fuggles Leaf Hops, leaf, Alpha: 3.4%

1/4 ounce wild hops picked at Pineview Lake, Utah, or Czech Saaz Hops

1. Add the hops and boil for 15 minutes. Turn off the heat and cool to 73 degrees. Add to two 6 1/2-gallon carboys. Aerate with straight oxygen for 50 seconds.

2. Pitch yeast starter made from Irish Ale Yeast. Leave at 70 to 75 degrees overnight, then store at 60° F for 2 weeks.

3. Rack into two 5-gallon secondary fermenters and let ferment for 3 to 4 weeks.

1 1/4 cups light DME and 2 cups water to prime each carboy for bottling

Original specific gravity: 1.053   Alcohol: 7.2%

Terminal specific gravity: 1.029   Alcohol: 4.0%

Final specific gravity: 1.017   Alcohol: 2.2%

Final alcohol: 5.0%

Bread & Rolls

Brød & Boller

The fact that bread is the staff of life seems as evident in Denmark as anywhere. Brød & boller—all various kinds—are served for breakfast, lunch, and dinner.

A staple of the Danish diet for centuries, rye bread enjoys continued popularity as the foundation for smørrebrød, open-face sandwiches. Its heavy dough may present a challenge, but a heavy-duty mixer or bread maker makes the task easier, and the results are well worth the effort.

For years, wheat bread was a luxury item available only to royalty, preists, and the upper classes. Not until the late 1800s did white flour become commonly available. Until then, most people ate the hearty whole-grain breads, made from flours we now realize are full of vitamins and minerals, much better for one's health.

Look over the following recipes. Try the one that appeals to you most. Then try another and another. They will all reward your time and effort. As the saying goes, "There's nothing better than a freshly baked loaf of homemade bread." The Danes have been proving this true for centuries.

Ham and Cheese Bread
Skinke og ostebrød

Makes 3 loaves

1/2 cup unbleached bread flour
1 tablespoon instant dry yeast
1 1/4 cups 2% milk
2 cups unbleached bread flour
1 1/2 cups whole wheat flour
1 tablespoon sugar
1 teaspoon salt
2 eggs, lightly beaten
3/4 cup (1 1/2 sticks)
    butter, softened
1 cup (1/4-inch pieces)
    chopped ham
1 cup (4 ounces) coarsely
    shredded Havarti cheese
3 garlic cloves, finely chopped

This is like eating an all-in-one sandwich, with the meat and cheese cooked in the bread!

1 Mix 1/2 cup bread flour with the yeast in a large mixing bowl. Heat the milk to 95 degrees in a saucepan and add to the flour mixture; whisk to mix well. Cover with plastic wrap and let stand at room temperature for 1 hour. The mixture will foam and bubble and will collapse when the bowl is tapped.

2 Mix 2 cups bread flour with the whole wheat flour, sugar and salt in a bowl. Add to the yeast mixture and mix well. Add the eggs and stir for 1 minute. Let the dough stand, covered, for 10 minutes to allow the gluten to develop.

3 Cut the butter into six pieces and work into the dough one piece at a time, mixing at medium speed for a total of 12 minutes; the dough will change from sticky to tacky and will leave the side of the bowl.

4 Add the ham, cheese and garlic and mix gently into the dough. Shape the dough into a ball on a work surface. Place in an oiled bowl, turning to coat the surface. Cover with plastic wrap and let rise at room temperature for 1 1/2 hours or until doubled in bulk.

5 Cut the dough into three pieces and shape into round loaves. Place in three well greased 6 1/2-inch round or square pans and spray lightly with cooking spray. Cover with plastic wrap and let rise for 1 to 1 1/2 hours.

6 Bake at 350 degrees for 25 to 30 minutes or until golden brown. Remove to wire racks to cool for 1 hour or longer.

Danish Blue Cheese Bread
Danish Blue ostebrød

Makes 1 loaf or 15 rolls

2 cups whole wheat flour

2 cups unbleached bread flour

3 tablespoons instant dry yeast

1 cup crumbled Danish
    blue cheese

3 eggs

1 tablespoon brown sugar

1 cup water, at room temperature

$1/2$ teaspoon salt

1 egg, beaten

1 Mix the whole wheat flour, bread flour and yeast in a bowl. Combine the blue cheese, 3 eggs, the brown sugar, water and salt in a mixing bowl and mix well. Add the dry ingredients and mix well. Knead on a lightly floured surface for 6 to 8 minutes or until smooth and elastic.

2 Shape into a ball and place in an oiled bowl, turning to coat the surface. Cover with plastic wrap and let rise at room temperature for $1^1/2$ hours.

3 Shape into a loaf and place in a greased 5×9-inch loaf pan. Cover with plastic wrap and let rise at room temperature for 1 hour. Brush the top with the beaten egg.

4 Bake at 350 degrees for 40 to 45 minutes or until golden brown. Remove from the pan to a wire rack to cool. Slice to serve.

Bolted Rye Bread

Sigtebrød

Makes 1 loaf

Sourdough Starter
1 1/2 cups light rye flour
1/2 teaspoon instant dry yeast
1 cup 1% or 2% milk

Bolted Rye Bread
2 1/3 cups light rye flour
1 teaspoon instant dry yeast
1 teaspoon ground fennel seeds
2 teaspoons salt
1/2 cup 1% or 2% milk

Sourdough Starter

Mix 1 1/2 cups flour with the yeast in a small mixing bowl. Heat the milk to 85 degrees in a small saucepan and add to the flour mixture; mix well. Cover with plastic wrap and let stand at room temperature for 24 hours for the sourdough starter.

Bread

1 Combine 2 1/3 cups flour, the yeast, ground fennel seeds and salt in a medium mixing bowl. Heat the milk to 85 degrees in a small saucepan and add to the flour mixture; mix well. Mix in the sourdough starter.

2 Knead on a lightly floured surface for 7 to 8 minutes or until smooth and elastic, but very firm. Place in an oiled bowl, turning to coat the surface. Cover with plastic wrap and let rise at room temperature for 4 hours; the dough will not change much in bulk.

3 Shape into a loaf and place in a lightly greased baking pan. Cover with plastic wrap and let rise for 30 minutes. Brush the loaf with water and place on the center oven rack. Bake at 350 degrees for 40 minutes.

4 Remove to a wire rack to cool for 15 minutes. Wrap with plastic wrap to give the loaf a softer crust; cool completely. Slice to serve with your favorite smørrebrød toppings such as Curried Herring* or Chicken Liver Pâté*. It is also good with Cream of Kale Soup*.

White Bread
Formfranskbrød

Makes 1 loaf

4³/4 cups unbleached bread flour
2 teaspoons instant dry yeast
¹/4 cup (¹/2 stick) butter, melted and cooled to room temperature
1³/4 cups water, at room temperature
2 tablespoons sugar
1 egg
¹/4 cup nonfat dry milk
1¹/2 teaspoons salt
1 egg, beaten

1 Mix the flour with the yeast in a bowl. Combine the butter with the water in a large mixing bowl. Add the sugar, 1 egg, the dry milk and salt; mix well. Add the flour mixture and mix to form a dough.

2 Knead the dough on a lightly floured surface for 5 to 7 minutes or until smooth and elastic. Place in an oiled bowl, turning to coat the surface. Cover with plastic wrap and let rise at room temperature for 1¹/2 to 2 hours or until doubled in bulk.

3 Shape the dough into an 8×8-inch square. Let stand for 5 minutes. Roll the dough tightly to form a loaf and place in a lightly greased 5×9-inch loaf pan. Cover with plastic wrap lightly sprayed with nonstick cooking spray. Let rise at room temperature for 1 to 1¹/2 hours or until doubled in bulk.

4 Brush the top with the beaten egg and cut a slit about ¹/4-inch deep lengthwise down the center with a sharp knife. Bake at 350 degrees for 40 minutes or until golden brown. Remove from the pan to a wire rack to cool. Cool for 1 hour or longer before slicing. Serve for smørrebrød.

Barley Bread
Bygbrød

Makes 1 loaf

1 cup cracked wheat
2 cups whole wheat flour
2 cups barley flour or unbleached bread flour
2¹/2 teaspoons instant dry yeast
1 (12-ounce) bottle of lager beer
2 tablespoons vegetable oil or olive oil
3 tablespoons honey
²/3 teaspoon salt
1 egg, beaten
¹/4 cup flaked or rolled barley

If barley flour is difficult to find, you can substitute unbleached bread flour, which actually rises better because of the gluten.

1 Place the cracked wheat in a small bowl and add enough hot water to cover. Let stand for 1 hour; drain. Mix the whole wheat flour, barley flour and yeast in a bowl.

2 Combine the beer, oil and honey in a microwave-safe bowl and microwave for 45 seconds or to 75 degrees. Add the drained cracked wheat, flour mixture and salt and mix well. Knead on a lightly floured surface for 5 to 7 minutes or until smooth and elastic.

3 Place in an oiled bowl, turning to coat the surface. Cover with plastic wrap and let rise at room temperature for 1¹/2 to 2 hours or until doubled in bulk. Shape into a loaf and place in a lightly greased 5×9-inch loaf pan. Cover with plastic wrap and let rise at room temperature for 50 minutes.

4 Brush with the beaten egg and sprinkle with the flaked barley. Bake at 350 degrees for 45 minutes or until the loaf tests done. Remove from the pan to a wire rack to cool. Cool for 30 minutes or longer. Slice to serve.

Scandinavian Rye Bread
Skandinavisk rugbrød

Makes 1 loaf

2 cups rye flour

2 cups unbleached bread flour

2 1/2 teaspoons instant dry yeast

1/4 teaspoon baking soda

3 tablespoons vegetable oil or
olive oil

3 tablespoons molasses

1 1/3 cups water,
at room temperature

1 1/2 teaspoons caraway seeds

1 1/2 teaspoons fennel seeds

1 teaspoon salt

1 Mix the rye flour and bread flour with the yeast and baking soda in a bowl. Combine the oil, molasses, water, caraway seeds, fennel seeds and salt in a mixing bowl and mix well. Mix in the flour mixture.

2 Knead the dough on a lightly floured surface for 8 to 10 minutes or until smooth and elastic. Place in an oiled bowl, turning to coat the surface. Cover with plastic wrap and let rise at room temperature for 1 1/2 hours or until doubled in bulk.

3 Shape into a loaf and place in a lightly greased 5×9-inch loaf pan. Cover with plastic wrap and let rise at room temperature for 45 minutes.

4 Place on the center oven rack and bake at 350 degrees for 45 minutes. Brush the top lightly with water and remove the bread from the pan to a wire rack to cool. Slice and enjoy with your favorite topping for smørrebrød.

Pumpernickel Bread
Rugbrød

Makes 1 loaf

2 1/2 cups whole wheat flour

1 1/2 cups dark rye flour

1 tablespoon instant dry yeast

1/2 teaspoon salt

2 cups buttermilk or 2% milk

3 tablespoons vegetable oil or
olive oil

1 teaspoon Kitchen Bouquet,
for color

1 Mix the whole wheat flour, rye flour, yeast and salt in a bowl. Place the buttermilk in a microwave-safe bowl and microwave for 1 minute or to 95 degrees. Stir in the oil and Kitchen Bouquet. Add the flour mixture and mix to form a dough.

2 Knead the dough on a lightly floured surface for 8 to 10 minutes or until smooth and elastic. Place in an oiled bowl, turning to coat the surface. Cover with plastic wrap and let rise at room temperature for 1 to 1 1/2 hours or until almost doubled in bulk.

3 Shape into a loaf, rolling the dough tightly. Place in a lightly greased 5×9-inch loaf pan. Cover with plastic wrap and let rise for 1 to 1 1/2 hours.

4 Bake the bread at 350 degrees for 45 minutes or until golden brown. Remove from the oven and brush the top lightly with water. Remove from the pan and cool on a wire rack. Slice to serve. This produces a soft pumpkernickel, which is great for a sandwich.

Grandpa's Pumpernickel Bread
Farfar's rugbrød

Makes 1 loaf

1 1/4 cups cracked wheat

3 cups rye flour

1 tablespoon instant dry yeast

2 teaspoons salt

1 cup water, at room temperature

1 tablespoon pancake syrup

1 tablespoon Kitchen Bouquet,
for color

1 1/4 cups buttermilk

1 cup unbleached bread flour

1 tablespoon melted butter

1 Mix the cracked wheat and rye flour with the yeast and salt in a mixing bowl. Combine the water, syrup and Kitchen Bouquet in a small bowl and mix well. Add to the dry ingredients and mix well.

2 Place the buttermilk in a microwave-safe bowl and microwave for 45 seconds or to 70 degrees. Add to the flour mixture and beat with the paddle attachment for 8 to 10 minutes, scraping the side of the bowl.

3 Cover with plastic wrap and let rise at room temperature for 1 hour. Mix or knead in the bread flour for several minutes and shape into a loaf. Place in a greased 5×9-inch loaf pan. Pierce the top lightly with a fork; the loaf will fall slightly. Brush with the melted butter.

4 Place on the center oven rack and bake at 350 degrees for 45 minutes or until the loaf sounds hollow when tapped. Remove from the pan to a wire rack to cool completely. Slice and serve with butter and your favorite smørrebrød toppings.

Pumpernickel Bread with Sourdough
Rugbrød med surdej

This bread is made with a sourdough starter rather than yeast.

Makes 2 loaves

Sourdough Starter

2 cups dark rye flour
1/2 teaspoon salt
2 cups buttermilk

Bread

2 cups unbleached bread flour
2 cups whole wheat flour
4 1/4 cups dark rye flour
2 teaspoons salt
4 cups water, at room temperature
3/4 cup porter or other dark beer
2 tablespoons brown sugar
3 cups cracked rye or
cracked wheat
2 tablespoons melted butter

Sourdough Starter

Mix the dark rye flour with the salt in a bowl. Add the buttermilk and mix well. Set stand, covered, at room temperature for 3 days.

Bread

1 Mix the bread flour, whole wheat flour and dark rye flour with the salt in a large mixing bowl. Add the water and mix well. Add the sourdough starter and mix to form a soft dough. Cover and let stand at room temperature for 8 hours or longer.

2 Place the dough on a floured surface. Combine the beer, brown sugar and cracked rye in a small bowl and mix well. Spoon into the center of the dough and work it in, kneading for 4 to 5 minutes and adding additional flour to the work surface as needed; the dough will be very soft.

3 Divide the dough into halves and shape into loaves. Place in two greased 5×9-inch loaf pans. Cover with plastic wrap and let rise at room temperature for 6 to 7 hours. Brush the tops with the melted butter.

4 Place on the center oven rack and bake at 350 degrees for 1 1/2 hours or until the loaves test done. Remove from the pans to a wire rack to cool for 1 hour or longer. Wrap in plastic wrap and store until the next day for ease of slicing. Serve for breakfast with butter, cheese and Raspberry Jam*.

As a teenager I worked one summer at Kanehøj Mølle, a pumpernickel bakery. The bakery was part of a flour mill that was built in 1680 and rebuilt two hundred years later. The mill continues to operate today and grinds mostly specialty flours for retail sale. Kanehøj is the Bronze Age mound nearby from which the mill takes its name. The mound served a more sinister purpose longer ago than the mill has been grinding out the staff of life. Still visible is the indentation in the earth that caught the decapitated heads of persons executed by public beheading. In 1825, the country's last public beheading was performed there. At the time, public executions were considered popular entertainment. In his autobiography, Hans Christian Andersen recounts his attendance at this event.

Cinnamon Raisin Walnut Bread
Rosinbrød

Makes 2 loaves

3¹/₂ cups unbleached bread flour

4 teaspoons sugar

2 teaspoons instant dry yeast

1¹/₄ teaspoons ground cinnamon

1¹/₄ teaspoons salt

1¹/₄ cups 2% milk,
 at room temperature

2 tablespoons unsalted butter,
 melted and cooled to
 room temperature

1 egg, lightly beaten

1¹/₂ cups raisins

1 cup chopped walnuts

1 tablespoon melted butter

2 tablespoons sugar

¹/₄ tablespoon ground cinnamon

1 Mix the flour, 4 teaspoons sugar, the yeast, 1¹/₄ teaspoons cinnamon and the salt in a mixing bowl. Add the milk, 2 tablespoons unsalted butter and the egg and mix well.

2 Soak the raisins in enough water to cover in a bowl. Knead the dough on a lightly floured surface for 6 to 8 minutes or until smooth and elastic. Drain the raisins and add to the dough with the walnuts. Knead for 2 minutes or until the raisins and walnuts are well incorporated.

3 Place in an oiled bowl, turning to coat the surface. Cover with plastic wrap and let rise at room temperature for 2 hours or until doubled in bulk. Divide into halves and shape into loaves in two lightly greased 4×8-inch loaf pans. Cover with plastic wrap and let rise at room temperature for 1 hour.

4 Place on the center oven rack and bake at 350 degrees for 35 minutes. Remove from the pans to a wire rack. Brush with 1 tablespoon melted butter and sprinkle with 2 tablespoons sugar and ¹/₄ tablespoon cinnamon.

5 Cool for 1 hour before slicing. Slice and spread generously with butter to serve. Great for making French toast the next day.

Breakfast Rolls
Rundstykker

Makes 12 rolls

4 1/4 cups unbleached bread flour

5 teaspoons instant dry yeast

1 tablespoon sugar

1 teaspoon salt

2 tablespoons butter, melted and
cooled to room temperature

1 1/2 cups (90-degree) water

1 egg

Poppy seeds

1 Mix the flour, yeast, sugar and salt in a large mixing bowl. Add the butter, 1 1/2 cups water and the egg and mix well. Knead on a lightly floured surface for 6 to 8 minutes or until smooth and elastic.

2 Place in an oiled bowl, turning to coat the surface. Cover with plastic wrap and let rise at room temperature for 30 minutes. Cut the dough into twelve equal portions and let stand for 5 minutes.

3 Shape the dough into rolls and dip the tops of the rolls into water. Press into the poppy seeds and arrange in a lightly greased 12×17-inch baking pan. Spray plastic wrap with nonstick cooking spray and cover the rolls. Let rise at room temperature for 30 minutes.

4 Place an empty baking pan on the top oven rack and preheat the oven to 475 degrees. Place the rolls on the center oven rack. Pour 1 cup of water into the top baking pan. Spray the sides of the oven with water. Close the oven quickly without slamming it. Wait a minute and repeat spraying. Bake the rolls for 10 minutes. Reduce the oven temperature to 425 degrees and bake for 8 to 10 minutes longer or until golden brown.

5 Remove to a wire rack to cool. Serve with butter, Raspberry Jam*, Havarti cheese and coffee or tea.

Rundstykker

In Denmark, rundstykker is traditionally topped with white poppy seeds, but they are difficult to find and the dark seeds taste just the same. Without a steam oven, this recipe is the closest you can get to a rundstykker with the traditional crisp crust, and the advantage is that these are just as good the second day.

Makes 24 rolls

Rolls

3 1/2 cups unbleached bread flour
2 tablespoons instant dry yeast
1/4 teaspoon ground cardamom
1 cup 2% milk
7/8 cup (1 3/4 sticks) butter
1/4 cup sugar
1 egg
1 teaspoon salt
1/2 cup raisins
1/2 cup chopped candied
    orange peel
Raspberry Jam* or other jam
    (optional)
Cream Filling* (optional)
1 egg, beaten
Sugar crystals (optional)

Frosting

1 cup confectioners' sugar
4 to 5 tablespoons hot water
2 tablespoons baking cocoa
1/4 teaspoon hot water

Rolls for Lent
Fastelavnsboller

These rolls are served on the first day of Lent, when the children go from door to door asking for a treat. Use a variety of toppings for the rolls, including jam, cream filling, crystal sugar and frosting, or just serve them plain.

Rolls

1 Mix the flour with the yeast and cardamom in a bowl. Combine the milk and butter in a microwave-safe bowl. Microwave for 1 minute or to 90 degrees. Add the sugar, 1 egg, the salt and the flour mixture; mix well.

2 Knead on a lightly floured surface for 5 to 7 minutes or until smooth and elastic. Add the raisins and orange peel and mix well.

3 Place the dough in an oiled bowl, turning to coat the surface. Cover with plastic wrap and let rise at room temperature for 1 hour or until doubled in bulk. Divide the dough into four equal portions and let stand for 5 minutes.

4 Cut each portion into six pieces and shape into rolls. Place in a lightly greased 12×17-inch baking pan. Make an indentation in rolls to be filled and spoon 1/2 teaspoon Raspberry Jam or Cream Filling into the indentations.

5 Spray plastic wrap with nonstick cooking spray and cover the rolls. Let rise at room temperature for 1 1/2 to 2 hours or until almost doubled in bulk. Brush with the beaten egg. Sprinkle rolls with sugar crystals.

6 Place the rolls on the center oven rack and bake at 425 degrees for 15 minutes. Remove to a wire rack to cool. Frost cooled rolls, if desired.

Frosting

Combine the confectioners' sugar and 4 to 5 tablespoons hot water in a bowl and mix well. Divide into two portions. Spread one portion of the frosting over some of the rolls. Add the baking cocoa and 1/4 teaspoon additional water to the remaining portion. Spread on the rolls.

Raisin Rolls
Rosinboller

**Makes 12 large rolls
or 20 small rolls.**

1¹/2 cups raisins
4¹/4 cups unbleached bread flour
2 teaspoons instant dry yeast
1¹/2 cups 2% milk
¹/4 cup (¹/2 stick) butter
3 tablespoons sugar
1 egg
1¹/2 teaspoons salt
1 egg, beaten

Raisin rolls are often served for birthday parties with hot chocolate as a snack before the cake.

1 Soak the raisins in enough cold water to cover in a small bowl. Mix the flour and yeast in a bowl. Combine the milk and butter in a microwave-safe bowl. Microwave for 1¹/2 minutes or to 100 degrees. Add the sugar, 1 egg, the flour mixture and salt; mix well.

2 Knead the dough on a lightly floured surface for 5 to 7 minutes or until smooth and elastic. Drain the raisins and add to the dough. Knead until the raisins are incorporated. Place in an oiled bowl, turning to coat the surface.

3 Cover with plastic wrap and let rise at room temperature for 1¹/2 to 2 hours or until doubled in bulk. Divide the dough into twelve portions for large rolls or twenty portions for small rolls. Shape into rolls and place in a lightly greased 12×16-inch baking pan.

4 Spray plastic wrap with nonstick cooking spray and cover the rolls. Let rise at room temperature for 1¹/2 to 2 hours or until doubled in bulk. Brush the tops of the rolls gently with the beaten egg.

5 Place the rolls on the center oven rack and bake at 400 degrees for 15 to 18 minutes or until golden brown. Remove to a wire rack to cool. Cut into halves and spread with butter to serve with hot chocolate.

Stuffed Sweet Rolls
Smørkage

Sweet Rolls

1 (4-ounce) package vanilla
    pudding and pie filling mix
3 cups 2% milk
1 tablespoon granulated sugar
1/2 cup (1 stick) butter
3/4 cup granulated sugar
1 1/2 teaspoons salt
2 eggs
5 1/4 cups unbleached bread flour
1 tablespoon instant dry yeast
1 3/4 cups 2% milk,
    at room temperature
1 1/2 cups raisins
1 tablespoon ground cinnamon
6 tablespoons granulated sugar

Orange Icing

3 1/2 tablespoons thawed frozen
    orange juice concentrate
2 cups confectioners' sugar

Sweet Rolls

1 Combine the pudding mix with 3 cups milk in a saucepan and mix well. Bring to a boil over medium heat, stirring constantly. Pour into a bowl and sprinkle with 1 tablespoon granulated sugar. Cool to room temperature.

2 Combine the butter, 3/4 cup granulated sugar and the salt in a mixing bowl and mix with the paddle attachment until light and creamy. Mix in the eggs one at a time. Add the flour, yeast and 1 3/4 cups milk; mix well.

3 Knead with the dough hook for 10 minutes. Shape into a ball on a lightly floured surface. Place in an oiled bowl, turning to coat the surface. Cover with plastic wrap and let rise at room temperature for 2 hours.

4 Divide the dough into two portions and shape into balls. Let stand for 5 minutes. Roll one portion into a 12×17-inch rectangle. Place in a greased 12×17-inch baking pan. Spread the pudding mixture over the dough and sprinkle with the raisins.

5 Roll the second portion into a 12×16-inch rectangle. Sprinkle with a mixture of the cinnamon and 6 tablespoons granulated sugar. Roll up tightly from the long side. Cut into twenty slices with a serrated knife.

6 Place the slices cut side down in the prepared baking pan, arranging them in five rows of four slices. Cover with plastic wrap and let rise at room temperature for 1 1/2 hours. Bake at 350 degrees for 45 minutes or until golden brown. Remove to a wire rack and cool for 10 minutes.

Icing

Add the orange juice concentrate gradually to the confectioners' sugar in a small bowl, stirring constantly until smooth. Brush over the rolls. Let stand for 20 minutes or until the icing is set. Reheat the individual rolls in the microwave for 20 seconds to serve warm.

White Rolls
Boller

**Makes 12 large rolls
or 20 small rolls**

4 1/4 cups unbleached bread flour
2 teaspoons instant dry yeast
1 1/2 cups milk
1/4 cup (1/2 stick) butter
3 tablespoons sugar
1 egg
1 1/2 teaspoons salt
1 egg, beaten
Poppy seeds or sesame seeds
    (optional)

1 Mix the flour with the yeast in a bowl. Combine the milk and butter in a microwave-safe bowl. Microwave for 1 1/2 minutes or to 80 degrees. Add the sugar, 1 egg, the flour mixture and salt; mix well.

2 Knead on a lightly floured surface for 5 to 7 minutes or until smooth and elastic. Place in an oiled bowl, turning to coat the surface. Cover with plastic wrap and let rise at room temperature for 1 1/2 to 2 hours or until doubled in bulk.

3 Divide the dough into twelve portions for large rolls or twenty portions for small rolls. Shape into rolls and place in a lightly greased baking pan. Spray plastic wrap with nonstick cooking spray and cover the rolls. Let rise at room temperature for 1 1/2 to 2 hours or until doubled in bulk.

4 Brush the tops of the rolls with the beaten egg and sprinkle with poppy seeds or sesame seeds. Bake at 400 degrees for 15 to 18 minutes or until golden brown. Remove to a wire rack to cool. Cut in half and serve with butter and Raspberry Jam*.

Horns

Horn

Makes 16 horns

4^1/$_4$ cups unbleached bread flour

2 teaspoons instant dry yeast

1^1/$_2$ cups 2% milk

^{1}/$_4$ cup (^{1}/$_2$ stick) butter

3 tablespoons sugar

1 egg

1^1/$_2$ teaspoons salt

1 egg, beaten

1 Mix the flour with the yeast in a bowl. Combine the milk and butter in a microwave-safe bowl. Microwave for 1^1/$_2$ minutes or to 90 degrees. Add the sugar, 1 egg, the flour mixture and salt; mix well.

2 Knead the dough on a lightly floured surface for 5 to 7 minutes or until smooth and elastic. Place in an oiled bowl, turning to coat the surface. Cover with plastic wrap and let rise at room temperature for 1^1/$_2$ to 2 hours or until doubled in bulk.

3 Divide the dough into halves and shape into balls. Let stand for 5 to 10 minutes. Roll each ball into a 12-inch circle, turning the dough over halfway through the process. Cut each circle into eight wedges. Roll up the wedges from the wide end and bend slightly to form a horn or crescent.

4 Place in a lightly greased 12×17-inch baking pan. Spray plastic wrap with nonstick cooking spray and cover the rolls. Let rise at room temperature for 1 to 1^1/$_2$ hours or until doubled in bulk.

5 Brush the tops of the rolls gently with the beaten egg. Place on the center oven rack and bake at 400 degrees for 15 to 18 minutes or until golden brown. Remove to a wire rack to cool slightly. Serve with butter and jam or as a delicious complement to Chicken Soup*.

Poppy Seed Triangles
Smørbirkes

Makes 10 to 12

3/4 cup (1 1/2 sticks) butter, chilled
    and finely chopped
3 1/3 cups unbleached bread flour
2 tablespoons instant dry yeast
1 tablespoon sugar
1 teaspoon salt
1 cup 2% milk
1 egg yolk
1/2 cup (1 stick) butter, softened
1 egg white, lightly beaten
3 tablespoons white or black
    poppy seeds

1 Add the cold chopped butter to the flour in a medium bowl and mix well. Mix in the yeast, sugar and salt. Microwave the milk in a microwave-safe bowl for 40 seconds or to 80 degrees. Add the milk and egg yolk to the flour mixture and mix well.

2 Knead the dough on a lightly floured surface for 4 to 5 minutes or until smooth and elastic. Place in an oiled bowl, turning to coat the surface. Cover with plastic wrap and let rise at room temperature for 30 minutes.

3 Roll the dough into a 10×24-inch rectangle on a lightly floured surface, turning the dough over halfway through. Spread the softened butter lengthwise over half the dough. Brush the beaten egg white in a 1/2-inch strip down the other long edge.

4 Fold the unbuttered side over the buttered side and tuck the edge brushed with egg white under, pressing to seal. Pierce the dough gently with a fork and brush with the remaining egg white. Sprinkle with the poppy seeds.

5 Cut the dough into ten to twelve triangles. Place in a 12×17-inch baking pan sprayed with nonstick cooking spray. Let stand for 10 minutes.

6 Place on the center oven rack and bake at 400 degrees for 18 to 22 minutes or until golden brown. Remove to a wire rack to cool for 15 minutes. Serve with butter, Raspberry Jam* and/or Havarti cheese.

Fruit Soup Biscuits

Kammerjunkere

Makes 56

1³/4 cups unbleached bread flour
1 teaspoon baking powder
¹/4 cup sugar
Pinch of cardamom
¹/2 cup (1 stick) butter, softened
1 egg
2 tablespoons water,
    at room temperature

1 Mix the flour with the baking powder, sugar and cardamom in a medium bowl. Add the butter and mix well with an electric mixer. Add the egg and water and beat at medium speed.

2 Roll the dough into a long rope 1 inch in diameter on a lightly floured surface. Cut into twenty-eight slices with a serrated knife. Roll each slice into a ball and arrange in a lightly greased 12×17-inch baking pan.

3 Place on the center oven rack and bake at 375 degrees for 12 minutes. Cool in the baking pan on a wire rack until cool enough to handle. Cut the biscuits into halves and return cut side up to the baking pan.

4 Reduce the oven temperature to 350 degrees. Place the baking pan on the center oven rack and bake the biscuits for 10 to 12 minutes longer or until light golden brown. Remove to a wire rack to cool. Store in an airtight container for several days.

5 Serve with hot or cold fruit soups, such as Rhubarb and Raspberry Soup* or Cold Buttermilk Soup with Strawberries*.

Inns of Denmark – Kroer i Danmark

When traveling in Denmark one place you are sure to find great traditional Danish food is in an inn. With more than 450 inns throughout Denmark, there are lots to choose from and more than 100 of them are established as a designated Royal Privileged Inn. These inns all have a great reputation for their restaurant and most of them also have overnight accommodations available.

Stop in for a cup of hot chocolate and delicious pastry on a cold winter day or in the evening for a large display of Danish delicacies for dinner.

Many of them date back to the 17th and 18th centuries and still have the traditional outside look and thatched roof; inside they are updated with all the modern conveniences while keeping the traditional look of the period in which they were built.

Danish Doughnuts
Æbleskiver

Makes 24 to 26

1³/₄ cups bread flour
2 teaspoons instant dry yeast
¹/₂ cup granulated sugar
¹/₂ teaspoon ground cardamom
¹/₄ cup (¹/₂ stick) butter
1 cup 2% milk
2 eggs
Shortening
Confectioners' sugar

You will need an æbleskiver pan to prepare these doughnuts. They can be found in many kitchen equipment stores and in Scandinavian import stores.

1 Combine the flour with the yeast, sugar and cardamom in a mixing bowl. Combine the butter and milk in a saucepan and heat to 70 to 80 degrees. Add to the flour mixture and mix well. Mix in the eggs. Cover with plastic wrap and let rise in a warm place for 1 hour or until doubled in bulk.

2 Heat an æbleskiver pan over low to medium (300-degree) heat. Add a small amount of shortening on the tip of a knife to each cup. Spoon the dough into the cups filling four-fifths full. Cook until the bottoms begin to brown and push one-fourth of the doughnut up to begin to brown the top. Repeat the process, then turn the doughnut completely over to form a ball and cook until golden brown all over.

3 Remove to a serving plate and sprinkle with confectioners' sugar. Serve with Raspberry Jam*, applesauce and sugar to dip in.

Æbleskiver

Æbleskiver has been a Danish favorite since the mid-1600s. They are traditionally served with a glass of gløgg at Christmas, but they are also served throughout the year at occasions such as harvest festivals and county fairs. The word æbleskiver translates as sliced apples, a name that comes from earlier times, when a slice of apple was added to the batter. The apple was dropped several hundred years ago and became the æbleskiver consisting of only the batter that we know today. In his 1858 cookbook, Frk. Jensen suggested that you place a piece of apple in the batter when it is ready to be turned. Æbleskiver are now available, frozen and ready to heat and eat, in markets in Denmark.

Entrées

Hovedretter

Although Danish meals typically open with soup, the hovedretter, the main dish, is the point of the meal. Conversation slows as everyone indulges in a filling dish of meat, poultry, or fish.

Pork is very popular in Denmark and is the main protein for many entrées. Fish is a close second, with chicken and beef following. I've included recipes for all of these, but there are many other meats Danes enjoy, such as rabbit.

Whichever it is, it will be an absolutely sensual delight and a filling experience. The scents, the flavors, and the warmth inside—these are what the main course is all about.

Breakfast

Morgenmad

Simplicity is the hallmark of the traditional Danish breakfast. It always features breads such as Breakfast Rolls*, Poppy Seed Triangles*, Breakfast Cake*, Pumpernickel Bread*, and Weinerbrød (Danish Pastry). Cheese, jam, coffee, and tea are also served. Oatmeal and Pumpernickel Beer Porridge* are popular hot selections. The recipe for Baked Eggs with Bread* included here is actually more of a lunch dish, but it works well for breakfast, too. Although you won't find hash browns or home fries on a Danish breakfast table, you may see hard-cooked eggs, yogurt, cereal, bacon, milk, and orange juice. Sometimes morgenmad includes a bitter such as Gammel Dansk—but be advised, this drink is 35 percent alcohol by volume!

Baked Eggs with Bread and Bacon
Æggekage med bacon

Serves 4

1/4 cup 2% milk
2 slices White Bread*
2 tablespoons butter
14 slices bacon
6 eggs
3 tablespoons 2% milk or
    half-and-half
1/2 tablespoon finely sliced
    fresh chives

1 Pour 2 tablespoons of the milk into each of two small plates. Place one slice of bread on each plate and let stand for 1 minute. Turn the bread over and let stand until all the milk is absorbed.

2 Melt the butter in an oven-proof skillet. Add the bread and cook until brown on both sides. Remove the bread to a plate.

3 Cook four slices of the bacon in the skillet until crisp. Drain on paper towels and reserve for the garnish. Cut the remaining ten slices bacon into strips crosswise. Cook in the skillet until crisp. Pour off two-thirds of the bacon drippings.

4 Beat the eggs with 3 tablespoons milk in a bowl until smooth. Add to the bacon in the skillet and cook until partially cooked. Lift the eggs gently from the bottom of the skillet to allow the uncooked eggs to run to the bottom of the pan.

5 Place the bread slices on the eggs and place the skillet in the oven. Bake at 375 degrees for 8 to 10 minutes or until done to taste. Cut into four wedges. Top each wedge with a slice of the reserved bacon and the chives.

Pumpernickel Beer Porridge
Øllebrød

Serves 4

10 ounces Pumpkernickel Bread*
5 cups cold water
1 cup porter or dark lager
1/3 cup packed brown sugar
Heavy cream or half-and-half,
    for topping
Whipped cream (optional)

Øllebrød is traditionally made with a dark thick nonalcoholic beer. It is only available in Denmark, but I find that a porter or dark lager works well. The pumpkernickel bread should be somewhat dry, but not stale.

1 Cut the bread into 1/2-inch cubes. Combine with the cold water in a medium saucepan. Cover and soak in the refrigerator for 8 hours or longer. Bring the mixture to a boil over low heat.

2 Reduce the heat and cover the saucepan. Simmer for 10 to 15 minutes, removing the lid to stir frequently to prevent sticking and burning and adding additional water if needed.

3 Press the mixture through a strainer or beat well to remove any lumps. Add the porter and brown sugar and bring to a boil. Boil for 5 to 8 minutes or until the mixture is the consistency of oatmeal. Ladle into serving bowls and serve with cream or half-and-half. Whipped cream in the center is a special treat.

Boneless "Birds"
Benløse fugle

Serves 4 to 6

1 1/2 pounds beef eye of round
3 thick slices bacon
1 1/2 carrots, peeled and cut into
    12 (3-inch) sticks
Ground pepper to taste
1/2 yellow onion, cut into
    1/2-inch pieces
2 tablespoons vegetable oil
1/4 cup tomato purée
2 cups water
2 tablespoons butter
3 1/2 tablespoons all-purpose flour
2 cups reserved cooking liquid
Salt to taste
1/4 cup heavy cream or
    half-and-half

1 Place the beef in the freezer for 2 to 3 hours for easy slicing. Cut the partially frozen beef into twelve 3/8-inch slices. Pound the slices with the fist on a work surface. Cut each bacon slice into four pieces.

2 Place one carrot stick and one piece of bacon on each beef slice and season with pepper. Roll the beef to enclose the filling and secure with kitchen twine or wooden picks.

3 Sauté the onion in the heated oil in a skillet over medium heat for several minutes. Add the beef rolls and sauté until brown on all sides. Stir in a mixture of the tomato purée and water.

4 Cover the skillet and simmer over low heat for 30 to 40 minutes or until the beef is cooked through, turning after 15 or 20 minutes. Remove the rolls to a serving plate, discarding the twine or picks. Reserve 2 cups of the cooking liquid for the sauce.

5 Melt the butter in a small heavy saucepan. Add the flour and cook over medium heat for 2 to 3 minutes, stirring constantly. Add the reserved cooking liquid gradually, bringing to a boil and stirring constantly. Season with salt and pepper and simmer for 3 to 4 minutes longer. Stir in the cream. Spoon the sauce over the beef rolls and serve with mashed potatoes.

Beef Hash
Biksemad

Serves 4

2 cups (^{1}/4-inch pieces)
    yellow onion
3 tablespoons butter or
    Sandwich Spread*
3 cups (^{1}/2-inch pieces)
    roast beef
3 cups (^{1}/2-inch pieces)
    boiled potatoes
^{3}/4 cup beef gravy
^{1}/4 cup ketchup
1 tablespoon Worcestershire
    sauce
^{1}/4 teaspoon pepper
4 eggs, fried to taste
Parsley

1 Sauté the onion in the butter in a skillet over medium heat for 5 to 8 minutes. Add the beef and sauté for 2 minutes. Add the potatoes, gravy, ketchup, Worcestershire sauce and pepper; mix gently. Simmer for several minutes, stirring frequently.

2 Spoon onto serving plates and top each serving with a fried egg. Garnish with parsley. You can substitute pork and pork gravy for the beef and beef gravy in this recipe.

Goulash
Gullasch

Serves 4

1 yellow onion, cut into
    ^{1}/4-inch pieces
3 garlic cloves, chopped
1 teaspoon caraway seeds
2 teaspoons Hungarian paprika
2 tablespoons butter
2 pounds lean stew beef,
    cut into ^{1}/2-inch pieces
^{1}/2 cup all-purpose flour
1 teaspoon salt
1 teaspoon pepper
^{1}/4 cup (^{1}/2 stick) butter
^{1}/2 cup beer
1^1/2 cups water or beef stock
^{1}/2 cup tomato sauce

1 Sauté the onion, garlic, caraway seeds and paprika in 2 tablespoons butter in a heavy medium saucepan until the onion is nearly tender. Remove the onion from the saucepan with a slotted spoon.

2 Coat the beef with a mixture of the flour, salt and pepper. Melt ^{1}/4 cup butter in the same saucepan and add half the beef. Cook over medium heat until brown on all sides; repeat with the remaining beef.

3 Combine all the beef with the onion, beer, water and tomato sauce in the saucepan and bring to a boil. Reduce the heat and simmer for 30 minutes or until the beef is cooked through. Serve with mashed potatoes.

Mock Turtle Stew
Forloren skildpadde

Serves 10 to 12

3 pounds beef rump roast or
    similar cut

4 carrots

3 celery ribs

1 leek

1/2 yellow onion

1 tablespoon salt

6 parsley sprigs

1 tablespoon peppercorns

6 tablespoons (3/4 stick) butter

1 cup all-purpose flour

1/2 teaspoon paprika

1/4 teaspoon cayenne pepper

1/4 cup tomato purée

1 teaspoon Kitchen Bouquet,
    for color

Salt and black pepper to taste

3/4 cup dry sherry

3 tablespoons brandy

1/3 recipe Danish Meatballs*

1 recipe Meat Dumplings*

1/2 recipe Fish Dumplings*

1/2 recipe Fish Dumplings*, fried

6 eggs, hard-cooked for 7 minutes
    and cut into halves lengthwise

This recipe makes a large portion, but because it freezes well it justifies the time and trouble it takes to prepare it. It is traditionally served with freshly baked puff pastry triangles, which can be made from frozen puff pastry.

1 Combine the beef with the carrots, celery, leek, onion, 1 tablespoon salt, the parsley and peppercorns in a large saucepan. Add enough water to cover and bring to a boil. Skim off any foam that appears on the surface of the water and reduce the heat. Simmer for 1 1/2 hours or until the beef is tender.

2 Remove the beef to a plate and bring the cooking stock to a rolling boil. Boil for 30 minutes to reduce. Strain the stock and reserve 6 cups; discard the vegetables. Cut the beef into 1/2-inch pieces.

3 Melt the butter in a large heavy saucepan. Add the flour, paprika and cayenne pepper. Cook over medium heat for 4 to 5 minutes, stirring constantly. Add the reserved 6 cups beef stock and bring to a boil, stirring constantly. Add the tomato purée and Kitchen Bouquet and season with salt and black pepper. Add the chopped beef, sherry and brandy and stir gently.

4 Prepare the Danish Meatballs and Meat Dumplings. Prepare the dough for one recipe of the Fish Dumplings and cook half the dough according to the recipe. Fry the remaining half of the dough by the method described for Danish Meatballs. Add half the Danish Meatballs, half the Meat Dumplings, half the Fish Dumplings and half the Fried Fish dumplings to the broth. Bring to a boil, stirring gently.

5 Spoon the stew into a large shallow serving dish and top with the remaining Danish Meatballs, Meat Dumplings, Fish Dumplings and the egg halves.

Egeskov Castle in Kværndrup on the island of Funen, was built in 1554.

Ground Beef Steak with Onions
Dansk bøf med løg

Serves 4

2 pounds lean ground beef
5 tablespoons all-purpose flour
¹/₄ teaspoon salt
¹/₈ teaspoon ground pepper
2 large onions, cut into halves and
    thinly sliced
6 tablespoons (³/₄ stick) butter
2 cups (about) water or liquid from
    boiling potatoes
1 tablespoon Kitchen Bouquet

1 Shape the ground beef into eight patties and crosshatch the tops with
   a knife. Mix the flour with the salt and pepper and coat the patties with
the mixture. Reserve the remaining flour mixture. Sauté the onions in half
the butter in a skillet until tender. Remove the onions with a slotted spoon.

2 Add the remaining butter to the skillet and add the beef patties.
   Cook over medium heat for 2 to 3 minutes; turn the patties and cook
for 2 to 3 minutes. Turn again and cook until done to taste. Remove to
serving plates.

3 Stir the reserved flour mixture into the drippings in the skillet and
   cook for 1 to 2 minutes, stirring constantly. Add the water and Kitchen
Bouquet. Simmer for 3 to 4 minutes, stirring constantly.

4 Spoon the gravy over the beef patties and top with the onions.
   Serve with boiled new potatoes, a fresh steamed vegetable and
Pickled Cucumber* or Cucumber Salad*.

Pork Tenderloin in Mushroom Sauce

Svinemørbrad i champignonsovs

Serves 4 to 6

Tenderloin

2 (18- to 20-ounce) pork
    tenderloins
Salt and ground pepper to taste
2 tablespoons vegetable oil or
    olive oil
5 cups sliced or quartered
    mushrooms
3 cups heavy cream or
    half-and-half

Sauce

2 tablespoons butter
3 1/2 tablespoons all-purpose flour
Reserved cream

Tenderloin

1 Trim the tenderloins of any fat and silver skin. Rub with salt and pepper. Heat the oil over high heat in a large heavy shallow saucepan. Add the tenderloin and brown on all sides. Add the mushrooms and sauté over high heat for 5 minutes, stirring the mushrooms and turning the pork frequently.

2 Stir in the cream and bring to a boil. Reduce the heat to very low and cover the saucepan. Simmer for 12 to 15 minutes or to 170 degrees on a meat thermometer, turning the pork occasionally. Remove the pork to a serving plate and keep warm. Strain the cream from the saucepan and reserve for the sauce.

Sauce

1 Melt the butter in a small saucepan. Stir in the flour and cook over medium heat for several minutes, stirring until smooth. Add the strained cream and bring to a boil, stirring constantly. Reduce the heat and simmer for several minutes.

2 Add the cream sauce to the mushrooms in the large saucepan. Bring to a boil and serve with the sliced pork, boiled potatoes and a green vegetable.

Castle Vacation – Slot's Ferie

Some of the old castles in Denmark have been converted into hotels and restaurants. It is truly an intriguing historical experience to stay in a castle like Dragsholm Slot in Hørve; this castle was built in the year 1200.

This huge castle has been renovated to become a hotel with all the modern-day amenities, while retaining the beauty of an 800-year-old building. The restaurant serves delicious, modern-style Danish food with an emphasis on the seasonal offerings.

Mock Duck
Forloren and

Serves 4 to 6

Tenderloin

2 (18- to 20-ounce) pork
   tenderloins
1 teaspoon salt
1/2 teaspoon pepper
1/2 Granny Smith apple, cut into
   1/8-inch slices
16 pitted prunes, cut into halves
2 tablespoons vegetable oil or
   olive oil
1 cup (about) merlot or other wine
2 cups (about) water

Sauce

2 tablespoons butter
3 1/2 tablespoons all-purpose flour

Serves 4 to 6

Tenderloin

1 Trim the tenderloins of any fat and silver skin. Make a lengthwise cut down
  the center of each tenderloin, cutting to but not through the other side.
Open the tenderloins on a work surface. Sprinkle with the salt and pepper.

2 Layer half the apple slices and half the prunes on each tenderloin.
  Roll the tenderloins from the long sides to enclose the filling; tie with
kitchen twine.

3 Heat the oil over high heat in a heavy shallow saucepan. Add the
  tenderloins and brown on all sides. Add the wine and water, adjusting
the amounts if necessary to measure a depth of 1/2 inch.

4 Bring to a boil, reduce the heat and cover the saucepan. Simmer for 15 to
  18 minutes. Remove the pork to a plate and keep warm, discarding the
kitchen twine. Reserve 2 cups of the cooking liquid for the sauce.

Sauce

1 Melt the butter in a small saucepan. Add the flour and cook over
  medium heat for several minutes, stirring until smooth. Add the reserved
2 cups cooking liquid and bring to a boil, stirring constantly. Reduce the
heat and simmer for several minutes.

2 Ladle the sauce over the sliced
  pork and serve as you would
roasted duck. Serve with Caramel
Potatoes*, Red Cabbage* and
Poached Apples*.

Caramelized Cabbage Braised with Pork
Brunkål med flæsk

Serves 4 to 6

1 head green cabbage
3/4 cup sugar
2 tablespoons butter
2 teaspoons salt
1/2 teaspoon ground pepper
1 1/2 pounds pork roast
1/2 cup water

Traditionally, this is made with pork belly, but that is very fatty and hard to find. You can use a pork shoulder, Boston butt, or a similar boneless cut of pork. If the cut is very thick, split it into halves for more even cooking.

1 Cut the cabbage into quarters, cutting through the core. Remove and discard the core. Cut the quarters into 1/4-inch slices.

2 Melt the sugar in a large heavy saucepan over medium heat. Cook until caramelized and golden brown. Add the butter carefully and cook until the butter melts. Add the cabbage and stir until well coated. Cook over high heat until the cabbage is brown. Season with the salt and pepper.

3 Remove half the cabbage from the saucepan. Place the pork on the cabbage in the saucepan and spread the remaining cabbage over the top. Add the water; cover and reduce the heat. Simmer over low heat for 1 1/2 hours or until the pork is cooked through, stirring gently several times during the cooking process.

4 Remove the pork to a plate and slice. Spoon the cabbage into a serving dish and arrange the pork over the top. Serve with Pumpkernickel Bread*.

Cabbage Rolls
Kåldolmere

Serves 4 to 6

Cabbage Rolls

1¹/2 pounds ground pork shoulder
    or similar cut
1 cup all-purpose flour
1 teaspoon granulated onion
2 teaspoons salt
1 teaspoon ground black pepper
2 eggs
1 cup 2% milk
1 head green cabbage
1 teaspoon salt

Sauce

¹/4 cup (¹/2 stick) butter
¹/2 cup all-purpose flour
1 cup heavy cream or half-and-half
Pinch of nutmeg
Salt and ground white pepper
    to taste

Rolls

1 Combine the pork with the flour, granulated onion, 2 teaspoons salt and the black pepper in a mixing bowl and mix well. Mix in the eggs and then the milk.

2 Remove the outer leaves from the cabbage and cut out the core. Place the cabbage in a medium saucepan and add enough water to cover. Add 1 teaspoon salt and bring to a boil. Simmer for 2 minutes and remove carefully from the hot water.

3 Peel away the outer leaves and reserve. Repeat the process until sixteen to eighteen partially cooked cabbage leaves have been removed. Return the leaves to the water in the saucepan and cook for 5 to 6 minutes or until tender.

4 Drain the leaves, reserving the cooking liquid. Cut out about 2 inches of the tough cabbage stems. Arrange the leaves on a work surface and spoon ¹/3 cup of the pork mixture onto each leaf. Fold the sides of the cabbage leaves over the pork and roll the leaves to enclose the filling.

5 Arrange the rolls in a buttered 9×13-inch baking dish. Add enough of the reserved cooking liquid to cover the rolls. Place on the center oven rack and bake at 400 degrees for 40 minutes. Remove from the oven and drain, reserving 3 cups of the cooking liquid for the sauce.

Sauce

1 Melt the butter in a small heavy saucepan. Add the flour and cook for 2 to 3 minutes, stirring until smooth. Add the reserved cooking liquid and cream. Bring to a boil, stirring constantly. Reduce the heat and simmer for 2 to 3 minutes, stirring occasionally. Season with nutmeg, salt and white pepper.

2 Pour the sauce over the rolls in the baking pan. Reduce the oven temperature to 350 degrees and bake the rolls for 10 minutes longer. Serve with boiled potatoes.

Mock Head Cheese
Forloren sylte

Makes 1 loaf

3 pounds pork shoulder or
    similar cut
1 tablespoon salt
4 bay leaves
5 whole cloves
1 teaspoon peppercorns
2 yellow onions,
    cut into halves
3/4 ounce unflavored gelatin
1/2 cup cold water

Head cheese is traditionally made with the meat from a pig's head. Pigs' heads are now hard to find and few people would be willing to go to the trouble of cleaning it; so I have given you a recipe made with pork shoulder.

1 Combine the pork with the salt and enough cold water to cover in a large heavy saucepan. Bring to a boil, skimming off any foam that rises to the surface. Add the bay leaves, cloves and peppercorns. Reduce the heat and cover. Simmer for 1 hour.

2 Add the onions and simmer, covered, for 2 hours or until the pork is very tender. Remove the pork and onions to a plate and strain the cooking liquid. Return the liquid to the saucepan and bring to a boil. Cook until reduced to less than 4 cups; measure 2 1/2 cups and reserve. Cut the pork and onions into 1/2-inch pieces.

3 Sprinkle the gelatin over 1/2 cup cold water in a large bowl. Let stand for 1 minute to soften. Bring the reserved 2 1/2 cups cooking liquid to a boil and pour over the gelatin, stirring to dissolve completely. Add the pork and onion and mix well.

4 Spoon the mixture into a 5×9-inch pan. Cover and chill in the refrigerator for 8 hours or longer. Loosen the edges with a spatula and dip the bottom of the pan in hot water. Invert onto a cutting board and cut into 1/4-inch slices.

5 Serve with Creamed Potatoes*, Red Beets*, Pumpkernickel Bread* and Mustard*, or use for a topping on smørrebrød.

Curried Pork

Svinekød i karry

Serves 4 to 6

Pork

1 large yellow onion
2 tablespoons vegetable oil or
  olive oil
2 pounds pork loin or similar cut,
  cut into $1/2$-inch pieces
3 cups water
1 Granny Smith apple, peeled and
  cut into $1/2$-inch pieces

Curry Sauce

1 (8-ounce) can pineapple chunks
$1/4$ cup (1 stick) butter
$1/2$ tablespoon curry powder
$1/2$ cup all-purpose flour
1 (13-ounce) can coconut milk
$1/2$ cup heavy cream
$1/2$ teaspoon salt
$1/4$ teaspoon pepper
$1/3$ cup shredded coconut
$1 1/2$ cups raisins
Toasted coconut

Pork

Cut the onion into $1/4$-inch pieces and sauté in the heated oil in a large heavy saucepan for several minutes. Add the pork and sauté until seared on all sides. Add the water and bring to a boil. Reduce the heat and simmer for 12 minutes. Add the apple and simmer for 5 minutes longer or until tender. Drain, reserving the pork, apples and cooking liquid.

Sauce

1 Drain the pineapple chunks, reserving the juice. Melt the butter in a small saucepan. Stir in the curry powder and sauté for 1 minute. Add the flour and cook for 1 to 2 minutes, stirring to blend well. Stir in the reserved cooking liquid, reserved pineapple juice, coconut milk, cream, salt and pepper.

2 Bring to a boil, stirring constantly. Reduce the heat and simmer for several minutes. Add the pork, $1/3$ cup coconut, the raisins and pineapple chunks. Bring to a boil and reduce the heat. Simmer until heated through. Ladle onto serving plates and sprinkle with toasted coconut. Serve with cooked long-grain rice.

Breaded Pork Patties

Karbonader

Serves 4 to 6

$1 1/2$ pounds ground pork
1 recipe Breading*
6 tablespoons ($3/4$ stick) butter

This recipe can also be prepared with boneless pork chops or ground veal, following the same recipe. For Krebinetter, a similar recipe, one part finely chopped boiled potatoes or carrots is added to two parts meat.

1 Shape the pork into six patties. Use the Breading recipe to dust the patties with flour, dip into egg and coat with bread crumbs. Melt the butter in a large skillet over medium heat. Add the patties and cook until golden brown on both sides. Reduce the heat and cook for 3 to 4 minutes longer.

2 Remove to a serving plate and drizzle the butter in the skillet over the top. Serve with Creamed Peas and Carrots* and potatoes.

Mock Rabbit Meat Loaf

Forloren hare

Serves 4 to 6

Meat Loaf

12 ounces ground pork
12 ounces ground beef
3/4 cup bread crumbs
1 teaspoon salt
1/2 teaspoon ground black pepper
3 eggs
1/3 cup heavy cream or
    half-and-half
5 slices bacon
3 cups 2% milk
2 teaspoons Kitchen Bouquet,
    for color

Sauce

1/4 cup (1/2 stick) butter
1/2 cup all-purpose flour
1/3 cup heavy cream or
    half-and-half
2 tablespoons currant jelly or other
    seedless jelly
Salt and ground white pepper
    to taste

Meat Loaf

1 Combine the ground pork and ground beef with the bread crumbs,
   1 teaspoon salt and 1/2 teaspoon pepper in a large mixing bowl.
Add the eggs and cream, mixing well after each addition. Shape into
a loaf with fingers dipped in cold water. Place in an 8×11-inch baking
pan. Top with the bacon slices.

2 Place the baking pan on the center oven rack. Bake at 475 degrees for
   20 minutes. Reduce the oven temperature to 350 degrees.

3 Mix the milk and Kitchen Bouquet in a bowl. Pour over the meat loaf.
   Bake for 40 minutes longer or to 166 degrees on a meat thermometer,
using a turkey baster to baste with the cooking liquid every 5 to 6 minutes.
Place the meat loaf on a plate; drain and reserve the cooking liquid for
the sauce.

Sauce

1 Melt the butter in a small heavy saucepan. Add the flour and cook over
   medium heat for 2 to 3 minutes, stirring until smooth. Add the reserved
cooking liquid and bring to a boil, stirring constantly. Reduce the heat and
simmer for 2 to 3 minutes. Stir in the cream, jelly, salt and white pepper.

2 Return the sauce to a boil and serve over the sliced meat loaf. Serve with
   potatoes and Picked Cucumber*.

Meatballs in Celery Root Sauce
Boller i selleri

Serves 4 to 6

1 1/2 pounds pork shoulder or
    similar cut, ground
1 cup all-purpose flour
2 teaspoons salt
1 teaspoon ground pepper
2 eggs
1 cup 2% milk
1 to 1 1/2 pounds celery root
1/2 teaspoon salt
2 tablespoons butter
3 1/2 tablespoons all-purpose flour
Pinch of nutmeg
Salt and white pepper to taste

Celery root is actually celeriac, which is a knobby brown vegetable available in better food markets in the winter months. If you purchase the pork ground, be sure that it is not seasoned pork sausage. Shape the meatballs into real Danish meatballs, or Frikadeller*.

1 Combine the ground pork and 1 cup flour in a mixing bowl and mix well. Add 2 teaspoons salt, the pepper, eggs and milk, mixing well after each addition. Spoon into a deep plate and chill in the refrigerator for 1 hour.

2 Peel the celery root and cut into 1/2-inch cubes. Combine with enough water to cover in a medium saucepan and add 1/2 teaspoon salt. Bring to a boil and reduce the heat. Simmer for 8 to 10 minutes or until the celery root is tender. Remove from the broth with a slotted spoon and reserve for the sauce. Bring the remaining broth to a boil.

3 Hold the dish with the pork mixture in the left hand and shape the mixture into balls with a spoon, spooning the meatballs directly into the broth and cooking in two batches if necessary. Cook the meatballs until cooked through. Remove the meatballs with a slotted spoon. Reserve the broth, adding milk if necessary to make 2 1/2 cups broth.

4 Melt the butter in a small heavy saucepan. Add 3 1/2 tablespoons flour and cook over medium heat for 2 to 3 minutes, stirring constantly.

5 Add the reserved broth, nutmeg, salt and white pepper. Simmer for 3 to 4 minutes or until thickened, stirring constantly.

6 Pour the sauce into a larger saucepan and add the reserved celery root. Bring to a boil and add the meatballs; mix gently and return to a boil. Serve with boiled potatoes or sliced Pumpernickel Bread*.

Danish Meatballs

Frikadeller

Serves 4 to 6

1 1/2 pounds ground pork shoulder
    or similar cut
1 cup all-purpose flour
2 teaspoons dehydrated onions
1/2 teaspoon granulated garlic
2 teaspoons salt
1 teaspoon ground pepper
2 eggs
1 cup 2% milk
Butter or margarine
Vegetable oil

If you purchase pork already ground at the market, be sure that it is not seasoned pork sausage. Danish Meatballs can be frozen and reheated in the oven or microwave.

1 Combine the ground pork with the flour in a bowl and mix well. Add the dehydrated onion, granulated garlic, salt and pepper. Mix in the eggs and then the milk. Spoon the mixture into a deep plate and chill in the refrigerator for 1 to 2 hours for easier shaping.

2 Add enough equal parts butter and oil to a skillet to measure 1/4 inch in depth. Heat over medium heat. Hold the dish with the meatball mixture in the left hand and spoon the pork mixture carefully into the pan with a soup spoon, shaping it into balls with the spoon. Cook the meatballs until brown on both sides, turning once.

3 Remove the meatballs to a plate. Serve warm with Red Cabbage* and Caramel Potatoes* or serve as a light lunch with Potato Salad*.

Frikadeller

Frikadeller is truly a favorite Danish dish that became very popular in the mid- to late-1800s, when many Danish farmers changed over to pork production. Bacon was sold on the English market for a good price and slaughterhouses were built all over Denmark, making fresh pork available year-round and not just in the fall, when pigs traditionally came to the market. With the invention of the manual meat grinder, ground pork became a product available to the average family, and frikadeller took the place of porridge, cabbage, and fish.

Pork Rinds

You will find the world's best pork rinds in Denmark! The butcher shops sell the delicious old-fashioned kind that are baked in the oven and still have a little fat on them. Because the entire pork roast still has the rind on it when you buy it in the butcher shop or grocery store, you get a delicious roast with the cracklings on top. You will have to watch the roast carefully to make sure nobody takes the cracklings before the dinner is served!

Danish Sausage
Medisterpølse

Serves 4 to 6

1 or 2 natural hog casings
3 pounds pork shoulder or
    similar cut, cut into
    1-inch cubes
2 teaspoons dehydrated onion
1 tablespoon salt
2 teaspoons ground white pepper
1 1/2 cups pork broth or water
1 teaspoon salt

The secret to success in making sausage is to tie a knot in the casings before filling them to make sure that no air gets into the casing.

1 Rinse the casings under cold water to remove excess salt. Soak in enough lukewarm water to cover for 1 hour or longer. Drain and rinse the casing inside and out.

2 Combine the pork with the dehydrated onion, 1 tablespoon salt and the white pepper in a medium bowl and mix well. Add the pork broth and mix well. Chill in the refrigerator for 1 hour.

3 Grind the mixture in meat grinder fitted with a coarse blade. Slip one casing over the stuffing horn and tie a knot in the end. Grind the meat mixture into the casing using the fine blade and using only enough pressure to fill the casing firmly without air pockets; the casing can burst during cooking if it is overfilled. Tie the end.

4 Bring a saucepan of water to a boil and add 1 teaspoon salt. Remove from the heat and add the sausage. Place over low heat and simmer for 15 minutes or until cooked through; do not boil. Drain and serve or pan-fry in butter until golden brown. Serve as dinner with Red Cabbage* and Caramel Potatoes*, as lunch with Potato Salad* or as a topping for smørrebrød.

Stuffed Onions
Farserede løg

Serves 4 to 6

Onions

4 to 6 large yellow onions
1 1/2 pounds ground pork shoulder
    or similar cut
1 cup all-purpose flour
2 teaspoons salt
1 teaspoon ground pepper
2 eggs
1 cup 2% milk

Sauce

2 tablespoons butter
3 1/2 tablespoons all-purpose flour
Pinch of ground nutmeg
Salt and ground white pepper
    to taste
3/4 cup heavy cream

Onions

1 Cut a small slice from the bottoms of the onions to help them stand. Peel off the outer layers of the onions. Cut a 1-inch slice off the tops of the onions and reserve. Scoop out the inside of the onions with a spoon, leaving the outer two layers intact. Cover the bottom with a piece of onion if the bottom comes out.

2 Combine the pork with the flour, salt and pepper in a medium mixing bowl. Add the eggs and milk, mixing well after each addition. Spoon the mixture into the onion shells and replace the tops.

3 Place the onions in a baking pan and add enough water to reach three-fourths up the sides of the onions. Cover loosely with foil and place on the center oven rack. Bake at 400 degrees for 1 hour. Remove the onions to a serving plate and reserve 2 cups of the cooking liquid.

Sauce

Melt the butter in a small heavy saucepan. Add the flour and cook over medium heat for 2 to 3 minutes, stirring until smooth. Add the reserved cooking liquid and bring to a boil, stirring constantly. Stir in the nutmeg, salt and white pepper. Reduce the heat and simmer for 3 to 4 minutes. Stir in the cream and return to a boil. Spoon over the onions and serve with potatoes and steamed fresh vegetables.

Fried Apples with Bacon
Æbleflæsk

Serves 4

16 slices bacon
1 small onion, diced
4 firm Granny Smith apples,
    peeled or unpeeled, cut into
      1/2-inch pieces
1 tablespoon sugar
4 slices bacon, crisp-cooked

1 Cut sixteen bacon slices into small strips. Cook the bacon strips in a large skillet over medium heat until crisp. Remove the bacon to a bowl, reserving the drippings in the skillet. Add the onion to the skillet and sauté until translucent; do not brown. Drain about half the drippings.

2 Add the apples to the skillet and sauté until tender. Stir in the sugar and return the bacon to the skillet; mix well. Cook just until heated through. Spoon into a serving dish and top with four bacon slices. Serve with Pumpkernickel Bread* and a cold porter.

Fried Bacon with Parsley Sauce
Stegt flæsk med persillesovs

Serves 4

12 to 15 white potatoes
1 teaspoon salt
20 to 24 slices thick slices bacon
1 recipe Parsley Sauce*

This is my mother's favorite dish. She tells me that when she was a child, her parents raised a pig every year. The bacon was salted and hung in the attic to cure.

1 Peel the potatoes and cut into large chunks. Combine with the salt and enough water to cover in a medium saucepan. Bring to a boil and reduce the heat. Simmer for 20 minutes or until tender.

2 Cook the bacon in a skillet until crisp. Drain and place on serving plates. Spoon the potatoes onto the plates and top with the Parsley Sauce. Serve with steamed vegetables.

3 You can reserve the bacon drippings to use in the Sandwich Spread*.

Burning Love

Brændende kærlighed

Serves 4 to 6

2 to 2¹/₂ pounds white potatoes
1 pound thick slices bacon
2 yellow onions, cut into
    ¹/₄-inch pieces
3 tablespoons butter
¹/₂ teaspoon salt
¹/₄ teaspoon ground white pepper
¹/₂ cup heavy cream or
    half-and-half
1 teaspoon chopped chives
1 cup (¹/₄-inch cubes) Red Beets*

I am not sure of the source of the name "Burning Love" for this recipe. It was used in Denmark long before Elvis used it in his song!

1 Peel the potatoes and cut into large pieces. Combine with enough water to cover in a medium saucepan and bring to a boil. Reduce the heat and simmer for 25 minutes or until tender.

2 Cut the bacon into thin strips. Cook in a skillet until crisp. Remove the bacon with a slotted spoon and add the onions to the drippings. Sauté until translucent and tender. Return the bacon to the skillet and keep warm.

3 Drain the potatoes and add the butter, salt and white pepper; mash until smooth. Add the cream and mix until fluffy. Spoon into a serving plate and make a well in the center.

4 Spoon the onion and bacon mixture into the well and over the top of the potatoes. Top with the chopped chives. Spoon Red Beets* around the edge of the plate and serve with Pumpernickel Bread*.

Hot Dogs and Potatoes

Svensk pølseret

Serves 4

1¹/₂ to 2 pounds potatoes, peeled
1 teaspoon salt
2 yellow onions, cut into
    ¹/₄-inch pieces
2 tablespoons butter
¹/₂ cup ketchup
³/₄ cup 2% milk
¹/₂ cup heavy cream
¹/₂ teaspoon ground pepper
7 or 8 hot dogs, cut into
    ¹/₂-inch pieces

This dish is also referred to as "Hurrah Sausage." It was typically served just before payday when money was short, so there might not be many sausages mixed in with the potatoes. Every time someone got a piece of sausage, he shouted "Hurrah."

1 Combine the potatoes with the salt and enough water to cover in a medium saucepan. Bring to a boil and reduce the heat. Simmer for 15 minutes or until tender but still firm. Drain the potatoes and cool; cut into ¹/₈-inch slices.

2 Sauté the onions in the butter in a skillet until translucent and tender. Stir in the ketchup, milk, cream and pepper. Add the hot dogs and potatoes and mix gently. Simmer until thickened.

Hot Dogs and All the Trimmings
Pølsebord

Serves 4 to 6

10 hot dogs
Butter
10 hot dog buns
1 recipe Potato Salad*
Remoulade*
1 recipe Cucumber Salad*
1 recipe Crisp Onions*
1 small onion, diced
Dijon mustard
Country-style Dijon mustard
Ketchup
Mayonnaise

Be sure to use a very good quality frankfurter-style hot dog.

1. Sauté the hot dogs in butter in a skillet over medium heat just until heated through or simmer in water in a saucepan just until heated through; do not overcook as the skins will split. Heat the buns in the oven; do not overheat.

2. Serve with the Potato Salad, Remoulade, Cucumber Salad, Crisp Onions, chopped onion, Dijon mustard, country-style Dijon mustard, ketchup and mayonnaise in separate bowls. Allow the guests to prepare hot dog to their individual tastes. Serve with a cold beer or soda.

Hot Dog Stands – Pølsevogn
When you arrive in Denmark at the Copenhagen CPH International Airport, you will see the first hot dog stand when you are no more that 100 meters from customs. It is a busy place from mid-morning until late at night. When you leave the airport, you will find them in cities throughout the country.

The Danes love their hot dogs, and for good reason—they are really great. Den røde pølse, the red sausage, was popular in Denmark for years, and it was almost a national catastrophe when scientists found that the red food color in the sausage is so bad for you that it was banned from food service use. No more røde pølser! Fortunately, a new red color was later found and the Danes have their røde pølser back.

Poached Cod

Kogt torsk

Serves 4

8 cups cold water
1/2 cup white vinegar
6 bay leaves
4 teaspoons salt
2 teaspoons peppercorns
4 fresh or thawed frozen
    (7- to 8-ounce) cod fillets
1 recipe Mustard Sauce*
1 lemon, cut into wedges

Kogt torsk is tradionally made using a whole cod and served for New Year's Eve dinner. Unfortunately, whole cod are almost impossible to find outside of Denmark, but fresh or frozen cod fillets can be substituted.

1 Combine the water, vinegar, bay leaves, salt and peppercorns in a medium saucepan and bring to a boil. Reduce the heat and simmer for 3 to 4 minutes.

2 Add the cod and return to a boil. Remove from the heat and cover the saucepan. Let stand for 6 to 8 minutes or until cooked through, depending on the thickness of the fish.

3 Remove the cod carefully to a serving plate. Top with the Mustard Sauce and lemon wedges. Serve with steamed asparagus.

Smoked Salmon
Varm røget laks

Serves 4

2 tablespoons sugar

1/4 teaspoon hot red
    pepper sauce

1 cup soy sauce or teriyaki sauce

1 cup lager beer

1/2 teaspoon granulated onion

1/2 teaspoon granulated garlic

3 tablespoons salt

1/2 teaspoon ground pepper

1 (2-pound) fresh salmon fillet

1 ounce each hickory wood and
    apple wood

Trout may be prepared in the same manner. Small trout may be smoked whole, while larger trout should be deboned.

1   Mix the sugar, hot sauce, soy sauce, beer, granulated onion, granulated garlic, salt and pepper in a glass dish, stirring to dissolve the sugar and salt completely. Rinse the salmon and pat dry. Place in the marinade and marinate in the refrigerator for 4 to 12 hours, turning at least once.

2   Remove the salmon and discard the marinade. Cut halfway through the fillet if using a tail piece and fold it under to ensure even thickness for smoking. Pat the salmon dry.

3   Prepare the smoker with the hickory wood and apple wood. Spray the rack with nonstick cooking spray. Place the salmon on the rack in the smoker and smoke at 200 degrees for 1 to 1 1/2 hours or until firm to the touch, depending on the thickness of the fish; do not overcook.

4   Remove the salmon from the smoker and discard the skin. Serve hot with boiled potatoes and steamed fresh asparagus or chill to serve later.

Fish Patties
Fiskefrikadeller

Serves 4 to 6

1 pound cod or similar fish

8 ounces salmon

5 ounces Smoked Salmon*

Salt to taste

2 teaspoons granulated onion

1 teaspoon granulated garlic

1 teaspoon ground pepper

2 tablespoons melted butter

4 egg yolks

3 1/2 tablespoons all-purpose flour

4 egg whites, beaten to soft peaks

6 ounces small shrimp

1   Sprinkle the cod and salmon with salt and let stand for 8 to 10 minutes. Pat the fish dry with paper towels. Grind the cod, salmon and Smoked Salmon in a meat grinder two times.

2   Combine the ground fish with the granulated onion, granulated garlic, pepper and butter in a mixing bowl and mix well. Add the egg yolks and flour and mix well. Fold in the beaten egg whites and shrimp.

3   Scoop into fifteen portions with a #16 ice cream scoop and shape into patties with hands dampened with cold water. Line a 12×17-inch baking pan with baking parchment and spray with nonstick cooking spray. Arrange the patties in the prepared pan.

4   Bake at 400 degrees for 35 minutes or until cooked through. Serve with boiled potatoes and fresh steamed vegetables topped with hollandaise sauce or Mustard Sauce*.

Traditional Danish Christmas Dinner

Greenland Shrimp Smørrebrød*

Ice-Cold Aquavit and Beer

Oven-Roasted Duck* Stuffed with Apple and Prunes

Roasted Whole Pork Loin

Sweet-and-Sour Red Cabbage*

Poached Granny Smith Apples* with Raspberry Jam*

Duck Sauce

Boiled Potatoes

Caramel Potatoes*

Pickled Cucumbers*

Pickled Red Beets*

Sweet Pickled Squash*

Freshly Baked White Rolls*

Red Wine

Rice Pudding*

Cherry Sauce*

Cherry Wine, Coffee and Tea

Assorted Christmas Cookies

Don't forget to add a whole almond to the Rice Pudding.
The person who finds the almond gets a prize.

Roasted Duck

Andesteg

Serves 4 to 6

Duck

2 fresh or frozen ducks
2 Granny Smith apples, peeled and
    cut into $1/2$-inch pieces
2 cups dried pitted prunes
Salt and pepper to taste

Sauce

$1/4$ teaspoon salt
1 teaspoon ground pepper
2 oranges
1 cup (about) all-purpose flour
Kitchen Bouquet, for color
$1/3$ cup heavy cream (optional)

Duck

1 Thaw frozen ducks in the refrigerator overnight. Remove and reserve the necks, hearts and giblets from the duck cavities. Rinse the ducks under cold running water. Remove and reserve the last joints from the wings; discard any excess fat.

2 Mix the apples and prunes in a bowl. Stuff into the duck cavities and secure the cavities with wooden picks. Season the ducks with salt and pepper.

3 Place the ducks in a roasting pan and add $1/2$ inch water. Place on the center oven rack and roast at 325 degrees for 1 hour. Roast for $2^1/2$ hours longer or until done to taste, basting every 15 minutes. Remove to a plate and tent with foil. Reserve the pan drippings for the sauce.

Sauce

1 Combine the reserved necks, hearts, giblets and wing tips with enough water to cover in a medium saucepan. Add $1/4$ teaspoon salt and 1 teaspoon pepper. Bring to a boil and skim off any foam that rises to the surface of the water. Reduce the heat and simmer for $1^1/2$ hours.

2 Cut the oranges into quarters and squeeze the juice into the saucepan. Add the orange rinds to the saucepan and cook for 15 minutes. Stir in the reserved drippings and return to a boil.

3 Strain the mixture into a heavy saucepan. Return to a boil and remove from the heat. Let stand until the fat rises to the surface. Sprinkle the flour on the surface and let stand until the flour is absorbed and falls to the bottom of the saucepan. Skim off any remaining fat.

4 Bring to a rolling boil and cook for 5 minutes, whisking constantly. Stir in the Kitchen Bouquet and cream. Return to a boil and keep warm.

5 Cut the ducks into quarters and cut the leg and thigh portions apart, reserving the stuffing. Cut the breasts into halves, if desired. Place on a serving tray and serve with the sauce, the apple and prune stuffing, Caramel Potatoes*, Red Cabbage*, Poached Apples* and Pickled Cucumber*.

Easter Leg of Lamb
Påskelammekølle

Serves 6 to 8

Lamb

1 fresh or thawed frozen
    leg of lamb
1 bunch parsley
2 garlic cloves, chopped
1 teaspoon salt
1/2 teaspoon ground pepper
2 cups mixture of chopped carrots,
    onion and celery
2 cups water
1 cup red wine
1/2 teaspoon salt
1/2 tablespoon black peppercorns

Lamb

1   Debone the leg of lamb or ask the butcher to do it for you; trim off excess fat. Open the boned lamb on a work surface and sprinkle with the parsley, garlic, 1 teaspoon salt and the ground pepper. Roll the lamb to enclose the filling and tie with kitchen twine.

2   Place the roast in an 8×11-inch roasting pan and add the chopped carrots, onion and celery mixture. Add the water, wine, 1/2 teaspoon salt and the peppercorns.

3   Place on the center oven rack and roast at 450 degrees for 20 minutes. Reduce the oven temperature to 350 degrees and roast for 1 to 1 1/2 hours or to 170 degrees on a meat thermometer, basting regularly with a turkey baster. Remove from the oven and tent with foil. Reserve 2 1/2 cups of the cooking liquid.

Sauce

3 tablespoons butter

5 tablespoons all-purpose flour

1/4 cup heavy cream

Kitchen Bouquet, for color

Salt and ground pepper to taste

Serves 4 to 6

6 cups whole milk

3/4 cup uncooked short grain
    pearl rice

1 teaspoon salt

Butter to taste

Cinnamon-sugar to taste

Sauce

Melt the butter in a small heavy saucepan. Add the flour and cook over medium heat for 2 to 3 minutes, stirring until smooth. Add the reserved cooking liquid and bring to a boil, stirring constantly. Reduce the heat and simmer for 3 to 4 minutes. Add the cream and Kitchen Bouquet. Season with salt and pepper. Spoon over the sliced lamb and serve with Cucumber Salad*, potatoes and other spring vegetables.

Rice Porridge
Risengrød

This was one of my favorite meals as a kid. It is also served with a dark, sweet nonalcoholic beer in Denmark. On Christmas Eve, many farm wives would put a pot of Rice Porridge up in the barn attic for the Julenisse, or Christmas Pixie, to enjoy. I am sure that the barn cats loved it!

1 Bring the milk to a boil in a heavy medium saucepan, stirring constantly to prevent scorching. Stir in the rice and return to a boil. Reduce the heat as low as possible and cover the saucepan. Simmer for 45 to 50 minutes, stirring regularly and taking care that it does not boil over. Stir in the salt.

2 Let stand for 15 minutes to absorb any remaining milk; add additional milk if the porridge is too thick. Ladle into serving bowls and top with butter and a sprinkle of cinnamon-sugar. Serve as an entrée or as dessert with a fruit punch. Use the leftovers for Rice Pancakes*.

Chicken Soup with Dumplings

Hønsekødsuppe

Serves 4 to 6

4 carrots
1/2 celery root
2 parsnips
2 leeks
1 large chicken
3 bay leaves
1/2 tablespoon salt
1 tablespoon peppercorns
1 recipe Meat Dumplings*, heated
1 recipe Dumplings*, heated
1 recipe Sweet-and-Sour Sauce* or
    Horseradish Sauce*
1/2 recipe Horns*

A hen is usually used for this dish in Denmark, where chickens are very small. In the United States a chicken works fine, or you can substitute beef for the chicken if you prefer.

1 Cut the carrots, celery root and parsnips into 3/8-inch cubes. Slice the leeks 1/8-inch thick. Reserve the vegetable trimmings for the broth.

2 Combine the chicken with enough water to cover in a large saucepan. Bring to a boil gradually, skimming off the foam that rises to the surface of the water. Add the bay leaves, salt, peppercorns and reserved vegetable trimmings. Reduce the heat and simmer for 1 hour or until the chicken is tender.

3 Remove the chicken to a plate; strain and reserve the broth, discarding the seasonings and vegetable trimmings. Combine the cut vegetables and the reserved broth in a saucepan and bring to a boil. Reduce the heat and simmer for 8 to 10 minutes or until the vegetables are tender. Adjust the seasonings to taste. Add the dumplings.

4 Ladle the soup into a soup tureen. Cut the chicken into eight to ten pieces and serve it on the side with Sweet-and-Sour Sauce or Horseradish Sauce and Horns*.

Yellow peas – Guleærter

The yellow peas that are so popular in Denmark are from a different variety of plant than the green peas more common in the United States. The yellow pea is a ripe seed that is available in both whole and split. Split peas are easier to work with as they boil easier for soup.

Yellow Split Pea Soup* is my father's favorite meal; it was always served on his birthday. Pea soup was popular long before his time, as the Greek and Roman street vendors were selling hot pea soup as early as 500 to 400 B.C.

Yellow Split Pea Soup
Guleærter med tilbehør

Serves 6 to 8

2 cups dried yellow split peas
2 cups cold water
2 leeks
2 carrots, cut into 1/4-inch pieces
1 parsnip, cut into 1/4-inch pieces
1/2 celery root, cut into
    1/4-inch pieces
3 pounds pork shoulder or
    similar cut
3 bay leaves
1/2 tablespoon salt
1/2 tablespoon peppercorns
1/4 teaspoon baking soda
1 cup pearl onions
1/2 teaspoon fresh or dried
    thyme leaves

1 Combine the peas with the water to cover in a medium bowl. Soak in the refrigerator for 8 hours or longer.

2 Cut the leeks into 1/16-inch slices and rinse in water. Set the carrots, parsnip and celery root aside; reserve any trimmings.

3 Combine the pork with water to cover in a saucepan; add any bones from the meat. Bring to a boil and skim off the foam. Add the vegetable trimmings, bay leaves, salt and peppercorns. Simmer for 1 3/4 hours or until the pork is cooked through. Remove to a plate; strain and reserve the broth.

4 Drain the peas and add to the reserved broth in the saucepan; stir in the baking soda. Bring to a boil and skim off the foam that rises to the surface. Reduce the heat and simmer for 45 minutes. Drain, reserving the broth. Press the peas through a strainer into a bowl.

5 Combine the leeks, carrots, parsnip, celery root and onions with enough water or broth to cover in a saucepan. Bring to a boil and reduce the heat. Simmer for 10 to 12 minutes or until the vegetables are tender.

6 Return the peas to a saucepan and add just enough broth or water to make a thick consistency. Bring to a boil, stirring constantly to prevent sticking. Reduce the heat and simmer for several minutes, stirring constantly.

7 Add the cooked vegetables and enough broth to make a semi-thick consistency. Season with the thyme and adjust the salt and pepper to taste. Heat to serving temperature. Ladle into soup bowls and serve with the sliced pork, boiled potatoes, Pumpernickel Bread*, Mustard*, and Danish Sausage*. Add a little vinegar or aquavit to each serving, if desired.

Side Dishes & Soups

Tilbehør til Hovedretter & Suppe

Denmark's chilly weather makes piping hot soup a popular choice for starting a meal. So hearty are these dishes that almost any one of them could stand alone as the centerpiece of a meal. Simply add fresh-baked bread for an easy dinner. I also included a couple of cold soups to enjoy during the warm summer months.

My dad calls soup "woman's food." To him, the entrée is the star of the show. And if the entrée is the star, the side dishes are the supporting cast, with the biggest supporting role in a Danish meal going to the potato! Danes eat potatoes in all their finest prepared forms imaginable, from elaborate to simply boiled and topped with a little chopped parsley. Nothing matches a Danish caramelized potato dish—don't even consider missing this one!

Pickled foods are also very popular alongside the entrée in Denmark: pickled sweet squash, green tomatoes, cucumber, and, of course, red beets. If there are no pickled delicacies on the table, then it isn't a true Danish meal!

Caramel Potatoes
Brune kartofler

Serves 4

1 cup sugar
2 tablespoons butter
1 (29-ounce) can small potatoes

If using small fresh potatoes for this recipe, boil them until about three-quarters done. Rather than using a spoon or spatula with sharp edges to stir the potatoes, use a wooden spoon to avoid cutting them because the caramel mixture will make dark lines in the cuts. The sugar is very hot as it caramelizes and will burn if it splatters and will melt a plastic spatula.

1 Sprinkle the sugar in a skillet and cook over low to medium heat until the sugar melts and turns golden brown, stirring constantly with a wooden spoon and watching carefully to prevent burning.

2 Add the butter and stir until the butter melts. Drain the potatoes, reserving 1/3 cup liquid. Add the reserved liquid carefully to the skillet and stir until the mixture is smooth. Add the potatoes and cook for 5 to 10 minutes or until golden brown, turning to coat evenly.

3 Serve with roasted pork, Roasted Duck* Danish Meatballs* or other meats.

Creamed Potatoes
Stuvede kartofler

Serves 4

5 or 6 white potatoes or other firm potatoes
1 recipe Basic White Sauce*, made with milk
1 teaspoon chopped fresh parsley

1 Combine the potatoes with enough water to cover in a medium saucepan. Bring to a boil and reduce the heat. Simmer for 30 minutes or until cooked through but still firm. Drain and cool the potatoes. Peel the potatoes and cut into 1/4-inch slices.

2 Heat the Basic White Sauce in a medium saucepan. Add the potatoes and mix gently. Simmer until heated through. Spoon into a serving dish and sprinkle with the parsley. Serve with Mock Head Cheese* or Danish Sausage*.

Potato Salad
Kartoffelsalat

Serves 4 to 6

4 white potatoes
4 eggs
$1/4$ green bell pepper
6 to 8 radishes, trimmed
$3/4$ cup mayonnaise
$1/4$ cup sour cream
1 tablespoon Mustard*
$1/8$ teaspoon dried thyme
$1/2$ teaspoon salt
$1/4$ teaspoon ground white pepper

1 Combine the potatoes with enough water to cover in a saucepan. Bring to a boil and cook for 20 to 25 minutes or until the potatoes are cooked through but still firm. Drain and place in cold water to cool. Peel the potatoes and cut into $1/4$-inch cubes.

2 Boil the eggs in water in a saucepan for 12 minutes. Drain and dice with an egg slicer, cutting twice. Cut the bell pepper into $1/8$-inch cubes. Cut the radishes into thin slices.

3 Mix the mayonnaise, sour cream, Mustard, thyme, salt and white pepper in a bowl. Add the potatoes and mix gently. Fold in the eggs, bell pepper and radishes. Chill in the refrigerator for several hours. Spoon into a serving bowl and garnish with sliced hard-cooked eggs and parsley.

Summer Salad
Sommersalat

Serves 4 to 6

6 white new potatoes
6 ounces cream cheese, softened
1 cup heavy cream
1 teaspoon salt
$1/2$ teaspoon ground white pepper
3 bunches radishes, sliced
    $1/16$-inch thick
1 cup thinly sliced
    European cucumber
2 tablespoons chopped chives

1 Combine the potatoes with enough water to cover in a saucepan. Boil until cooked through but still firm. Drain, cool and peel the potatoes. Chill in the refrigerator for 1 hour.

2 Combine the cream cheese, cream, salt and white pepper in a mixing bowl and beat with an electric mixture until the consistency of mayonnaise. Cut the potatoes into $1/8$-inch slices. Add the potatoes, radishes, cucumber and chives to the cream cheese mixture and mix gently with a spoon.

3 Place in a serving dish and chill in the refrigerator for several hours before serving. Serve with Danish Meatballs* or other meat dishes.

Red Cabbage

Rødkål

Serves 6 to 8

1 (2¹/₂- to 3-pound) red cabbage
1¹/₂ cups sugar
2 teaspoons salt
1 cup white vinegar
1 cup Raspberry Jam*, lingonberry
   jam or Cranberry Sauce*

1 Trim off the outer cabbage leaves; cut the cabbage into quarters and trim out the core. Cut the quarters into thin slices. Place in a large saucepan and add enough water to reach 1 inch below the level of the cabbage; the cabbage will reduce in bulk as it cooks.

2 Bring the cabbage to a boil and reduce the heat. Simmer for 45 minutes. Add the sugar, salt, vinegar and Raspberry Jam. Simmer for 15 minutes longer or until the cabbage is tender. Adjust the sugar or vinegar to taste.

3 Spoon into a serving bowl and garnish with an orange twist. Serve with Danish Meatballs* or as a topping for smørrebrød. Leftover cabbage freezes well. Add duck fat for flavor if it is available.

Creamed Peas and Carrots
Stuvede ærter og gulerødder

Serves 4 to 6

2 cups (1/2-inch pieces)
   peeled carrots
2 cups frozen peas
1 recipe Basic White Sauce*

1 Combine the carrots with enough water to cover by 1 inch in a heavy
   saucepan. Bring to a boil and reduce the heat. Simmer for 8 minutes.
Add the peas and return to a boil. Cook for 1 minute. Drain in a strainer.
2 Combine the peas and carrots with the Basic White Sauce in the
   saucepan and mix gently. Bring to a boil and reduce the heat. Simmer
for 1 to 2 minutes or until heated through. Serve with Breaded Pork Patties*
or other meat dishes.

Poached Apples
Pocherede æbler

Serves 6

3 Granny Smith apples or other
   tart firm apples
3 cups (about) water
1/2 cup (about) sugar
1 teaspoon (about) yellow
   food coloring
6 teaspoons Raspberry Jam*

1 Peel the apples and cut into halves horizontally. Scoop out the cores
   with a round teaspoon or melon baller. Add the water to a medium
saucepan, making sure that it is enough to float the apples. Add the sugar
and mix until the sugar dissolves. Add enough food coloring to color the
water bright yellow.
2 Bring the mixture to a boil and add the apples. Simmer for 5 minutes
   or until tender, turning several times. Remove the apples to a serving
plate with a slotted spoon. Fill the center of each apple with 1 teaspoon
Raspberry Jam. Serve with Roast Duck*, Mock Duck*, chicken or pork.

The island of Funen – Fyn
*The island of Funen is the third largest island in Denmark and is situated
more or less in the center of the country. Funen is the island where
I was born; it is also the island where the famous children's storybook
author Hans Christian Andersen was born, in the city of Odense.
With its beautiful countryside, thatched cottages, and bountiful farm
land he called this Denmark's Garden.*

   *In 1875 Hans Christian Andersen wrote this verse as a declaration
for his love of Funen:*
   Funen,
   Where I was born to the thoughts of light,
   between wild roses and the smell of hops.
   Blessed be your sunshine,
   Blessed be your air!

Pickling
Syltning

At one time, small family-based agriculture formed the backbone of Danish society. People made do with the food they could produce themselves or purchase locally. Long winters and a lack of refrigeration meant it was important to devise ways of storing food for a long time. Pickling had the advantage of preserving food and adding flavor to it at the same time.

Many forms of pickling are still popular in Denmark and enhance both hot, cooked dishes and open-face sandwiches.

The recipes offered here are a taste of tradition and a kick of flavor that will add zest to any meal. Be sure to make enough! An old Danish saying describes a get-together that falls short of expectations: "It was a great party but there weren't enough red beets."

Pickled Red Beets
Syltede rødbeder

Serves 20 to 22

Smaller beets are more tender and tastier for this recipe. Choose beets that are uniform in size so that they will cook evenly.

Marinade

4 cups white vinegar
3 cups sugar
2 cups pearl onions
5 garlic cloves
$1/2$ tablespoon peppercorns

Marinade
Combine the vinegar, sugar, pearl onions, garlic and peppercorns in a small saucepan. Bring to a boil and reduce the heat. Simmer for 3 to 4 minutes.

Beets

20 small red beets, about
    4 pounds
1 teaspoon salt

Beets

1 Cut off the green beet tops, leaving 1 inch of the stems and the root portion. Combine with the salt and enough cold water to cover. Bring to a boil and reduce the heat. Simmer for $1 1/2$ hours or until the beets are tender. Drain the beets and rinse with cold water. Let stand until cool enough to handle.

2 Press the beets to remove and discard the skins. Trim the roots and top. Cut into $1/8$-inch slices and place in a sterilized container.

3 Pour the marinade over the beets. Marinate, covered, in the refrigerator for at least 2 to 3 weeks before serving. Store in the refrigerator for up to 1 year. Serve with Chicken Liver Pâté*, Mock Head Cheese* or smørrebrød.

Cucumber Salad
Agurkesalat

Serves 6 to 8

European cucumbers are also known as hothouse cucumbers. They will last in the refrigerator for 8 to 10 days.

$1/2$ cup white vinegar
$1/2$ cup sugar
20 peppercorns
1 European cucumber
1 tablespoon salt

1 Combine the vinegar, sugar and peppercorns in a small saucepan. Heat just until the sugar dissolves, stirring to blend well. Spoon into a bowl and place in the refrigerator to chill.

2 Slice the cucumber very thin with a sharp knife or the slicing side of a cheese grater. Place in a bowl and sprinkle with salt; mix well. Chill in the refrigerator for 1 hour.

3 Squeeze the cucumber slices one handful at a time to remove the excess moisture, discarding the juice. Add to the vinegar mixture and mix well. Marinate in the refrigerator for several hours. Serve with roast chicken or pork, on smørrebrød or with Chicken Liver Pâté*.

Pickled Cucumber
Syltede asier

Serves 30 to 40

5 large cucumbers
Salt
4 cups white vinegar
3 cups sugar
1 pound pearl onions
3 red jalapeño chiles
2 bay leaves
1 teaspoon peppercorns

This can be made with extra-large late-season cucumbers!

1 Peel the cucumbers and cut into halves lengthwise. Scrape out the seeds with a spoon and discard. Sprinkle inside and out with salt. Let stand in the refrigerator for 8 hours or longer. Pat the salt off the cucumbers with paper towels and place in a glass dish.

2 Combine the vinegar and sugar in a saucepan and bring to a boil. Add the onions, jalapeño chiles, bay leaves and peppercorns. Reduce the heat and simmer for 3 to 4 minutes. Pour over the cucumbers.

3 Marinate in the refrigerator for 3 days. Drain the liquid into a saucepan and bring to a boil. Reduce the heat and simmer for 20 minutes. Cool completely. Pour over the cucumbers and marinate in the refrigerator for several days before serving. Store in the refrigerator for up to 1 year. Discard the bay leaves before serving.

Sweet Pickled Squash
Syltede græskar

Serves 30 to 40

4 pounds peeled and halved
    banana squash
2 cups white vinegar
2 cups water
6 cups sugar
2 cinnamon sticks
3 tablespoons vanilla extract

1 Cut the squash into 3/8-inch slices. Combine one-third at a time with enough water to cover in a saucepan. Cook until tender. Remove each batch with a slotted spoon and repeat the process with the remaining squash.

2 Combine the vinegar, water, sugar, cinnamon sticks and vanilla in a saucepan. Bring to a boil and reduce the heat. Simmer for 2 to 3 minutes. Add the squash one-third at a time and return to a boil. Reduce the heat and simmer for 10 to 12 minutes. Remove each batch to a sealable container with a slotted spoon and repeat with the remaining squash.

3 Boil the remaining liquid for 10 minutes or until reduced by one-fourth. Pour over the squash and seal. Marinate in the refrigerator for 2 weeks before serving. Store in the refrigerator for up to 1 year. Serve with roast beef, roasted chicken or Chicken Liver Pâté*

Pickled Green Tomatoes
Syltede grønne tomater

Serves 10 to 12

2 pounds green tomatoes
2 cups water
2 cups white vinegar
1 tablespoon salt
1/2 cup white vinegar
1/2 cup water
3 1/2 cups sugar
1 tablespoon vanilla extract

Use only fresh young tomatoes for this recipe. Late-season tomatoes will be too tough.

1 Cut out the stems of the tomatoes and cut an X in the bottoms. Bring the 2 cups water, 2 cups vinegar and the salt to a boil in a saucepan. Add the tomatoes and boil for 2 to 3 minutes or until the skins slip off easily. Remove the tomato skins and discard the hot liquid.

2 Combine 1/2 cup vinegar, 1/2 cup water, the sugar and vanilla in a saucepan. Bring to a boil and add the tomatoes. Reduce the heat and simmer for 2 to 3 minutes. Let stand for 8 to 12 hours. Return to a boil and reduce the heat. Simmer for 2 to 3 minutes.

3 Remove the tomatoes to a sterilized jar with a slotted spoon. Return the liquid to a boil and cook for 15 minutes to reduce. Pour over the tomatoes. Seal with a tight lid and store in the refrigerator for 2 weeks before serving. May be stored in the refrigerator for up to 1 year.

Mustard
Sennep

Makes about 3 cups

1 large yellow onion,
    finely chopped
3 garlic cloves, finely chopped
2 cups dry white wine
1 cup dry mustard
1/4 cup honey
4 teaspoons vegetable oil
2 teaspoons white wine
    vinegar
1 teaspoon salt

1 Combine the onion and garlic with the wine in a small saucepan. Bring to a boil and reduce the heat. Simmer for 5 to 8 minutes. Strain the wine into a bowl and discard the onion and garlic.

2 Add the dry mustard to the wine and whisk until smooth. Whisk in the honey, oil, vinegar and salt. Return the mixture to the saucepan and bring to a simmer over low heat, stirring constantly. Simmer for 1 to 2 minutes or until slightly thickened, stirring constantly.

3 Spoon into a glass container and cool in the refrigerator. Cover and chill for 2 days to blend the flavors. Store in the refrigerator for up to 1 month; the mustard will begin to lose its flavor after that.

Cranberry Sauce
Tranebærkompot

Makes 3 pints

3 oranges
3 (12-ounce) packages
    fresh cranberries
3 cups water
3 cinnamon sticks
3 cups sugar
1 teaspoon vanilla extract

Cranberries contain a natural preservative, so none is needed for this recipe.

1 Cut the zest from the oranges, taking care not to get any of the white pith. Squeeze the oranges and measure 1 1/2 cups juice. Combine the orange zest and orange juice with the cranberries, water and cinnamon sticks in a heavy medium saucepan. Bring to a boil and reduce the heat. Cover the saucepan and simmer for 20 minutes.

2 Add the sugar and vanilla and return to a boil. Reduce the heat and simmer, covered, for 5 minutes longer, skimming off any foam that rises to the surface.

3 Sterilize three 1-pint fruit jars in boiling water in a saucepan for 15 minutes; drain. Spoon the cranberry mixture into the jars. Place one cinnamon stick in each jar. Seal the jars tightly. Let stand for 1 hour to cool. Store in the refrigerator for 3 to 4 months. Serve with roasted poultry or pork.

Plum Chutney
Blommechutney

Makes 2 pints

8 ounces pearl onions,
cut into quarters

2 cups apple cider vinegar

1 small green, red or yellow bell
pepper, cut into 1-inch pieces

3/4 cup raisins, coarsely chopped

2 or 3 garlic cloves, pressed or
finely chopped

1/2 tablespoon finely
chopped fresh ginger

1/3 cup sugar

1 teaspoon salt

1/4 teaspoon ground
cayenne pepper

5 firm red plums, pitted and
cut into eights

10 firm Italian prune plums, pitted
and cut into quarters

1 Combine the onions and vinegar in a medium saucepan. Bring to a boil and reduce the heat. Cover the saucepan and simmer for 15 minutes. Add the bell pepper, raisins, garlic and ginger. Cook, covered, for 30 minutes, adding additional water if needed.

2 Stir in the sugar, salt and cayenne pepper. Add the plums and mix well. Return to a boil and reduce the heat. Simmer, covered, for 30 minutes, stirring several times.

3 Spoon into two sterilized 1-pint jars and seal tightly. Let stand until cool and store in the refrigerator for 1 week before serving. Serve with roasted pork, roasted chicken or Breaded Pork Chops*.

Raspberry Jam
Hindbærsyltetøj

Makes 3 quarts

2.2 pounds fresh raspberries, or
4 cups when mashed

8 cups sugar

2 envelopes pectin

1/4 cup lemon juice

It is important to use exact measurements of all ingredients for success with jam.

1 Crush the raspberries one cup at a time with a potato masher in a bowl. Measure 4 cups of the crushed berries and place in a bowl. Add the sugar one cup at a time, mixing well after each addition. Let stand for 10 minutes, stirring occasionally.

2 Combine the pectin with the lemon juice in a small bowl. Add to the raspberry mixture and stir for 3 minutes or until all the sugar is dissolved. Spoon the mixture into three sealable 1-quart freezer bags.

3 Let stand at room temperature for 24 hours or until set. Store in the freezer for up to 1 year. Thaw in the refrigerator to use. Serve on fresh White Rolls*.

Breading
Panere

Makes enough for 4 servings

2 eggs
1/2 tablespoon water
1/2 cup all-purpose flour
1 cup unseasoned bread crumbs

Combine the eggs with the water in a bowl and whisk to blend well. Place the flour and bread crumbs in separate bowls. Dip the item to be breaded into the flour. Dip in the egg wash and then into the bread crumbs, coating evenly; pat the bread crumbs to adhere well. Use this method for breading meat, poultry or fish.

Basic White Sauce
Grundlag hvid sovs

Serves 4 to 6

2 tablespoons butter
3 1/2 tablespoons all-purpose flour
2 cups chicken stock, beef stock
    or milk
Salt and ground white pepper
    to taste

Melt the butter in a small heavy saucepan over medium heat. Add the flour and cook for 2 to 3 minutes, stirring to blend well. Add the stock gradually and bring to a boil, stirring constantly. Reduce the heat and simmer for 3 or 4 minutes. Season with salt and white pepper to taste.

Sweet-and-Sour Sauce
Sur-sød sovs

Serves 4 to 6

1 recipe Basic White Sauce*
1 tablespoon white vinegar
1 tablespoon sugar

Heat the Basic White Sauce to a simmer in a saucepan. Add the vinegar and sugar and mix well. Adjust the vinegar and sugar to taste. Return to a simmer.

Sweet-and-Sour Horseradish Sauce
Sur-sød peberrodsovs

Serves 4 to 6

1 recipe Basic White Sauce*
1 tablespoon grated
   fresh horseradish
1 teaspoon white vinegar
1 teaspoon sugar

Heat the Basic White Sauce to a simmer in a saucepan. Add the horseradish, vinegar and sugar and mix well. Adjust the horseradish, vinegar and sugar to taste. Return to a simmer.

Parsley Sauce
Persillesovs

Serves 4 to 6

1 recipe Basic White Sauce*
1/3 bunch parsley, finely
    chopped

Heat the Basic White Sauce to a simmer in a saucepan. Add the parsley and simmer for 1 minute.

Asparagus Sauce
Aspargessovs

Serves 4 to 6

1 cup (1/4-inch pieces)
    fresh asparagus
Chicken stock
1 recipe Basic White Sauce* made
    with milk and asparagus
    cooking liquid

1 Cook the asparagus in a small amount of chicken stock for 8 minutes and drain, reserving the cooking liquid. Substitute the reserved cooking liquid for some of the milk when making the Basic White Sauce.

2 Add the asparagus to the Basic White Sauce in a saucepan and bring to a simmer. Simmer until heated through. You can also use canned asparagus and the drained liquid from the can for this recipe.

Danish Mustard Sauce
Fiskesennepsovs

Serves 4 to 6

2 tablespoons (or more) dry
    Danish mustard
1/4 cup cold water
1 recipe Basic White Sauce*
1/2 teaspoon white vinegar
1/2 teaspoon sugar

The Danish mustard used is Fiske-Sennepsmel, which can be purchased in Scandinavian import stores.

Mix the dry mustard with the cold water in a bowl. Let stand for 15 minutes. Bring the Basic White Sauce to a simmer in a saucepan. Stir in the vinegar and sugar. Return to a simmer and remove from the heat. Stir in the mustard mixture.

Mushroom Sauce
Champignonsovs

Serves 4 to 6

2 cups thinly sliced mushrooms
1 tablespoon butter
1 recipe Basic White Sauce*
1 tablespoon dry sherry

Sauté the mushrooms in the butter in a skillet until tender. Heat the Basic White Sauce to a simmer in a saucepan. Add the mushrooms and sherry and mix gently. Return to a simmer and cook until heated through.

Dumplings for Soup
Melboller

Serves 4 to 6 with soup

5 tablespoons butter
1/2 teaspoon salt
1 cup water
3/4 cup unbleached bread flour
2 eggs, beaten
1/2 teaspoon salt

A special soup dumpling shaper is available in Denmark, but a pastry bag, as suggested in this recipe, works just fine. Rinse the bag with cold water before filling for easy cleanup.

1 Combine the butter, 1/2 teaspoon salt and 1 cup water in a heavy small pan and bring to a boil over medium heat. Add the flour gradually, stirring constantly with a wooden spoon. Cook for 2 to 3 minutes, stirring constantly. Cool in the saucepan for several minutes. Add the beaten eggs to the dough gradually, mixing well after each addition.

2 Spoon the dough into a large pastry bag without a tip. Add 3 inches water to a medium saucepan and stir in 1/2 teaspoon salt. Bring to a boil and remove from the heat. Squeeze the dough from the pastry bag into the saucepan, cutting into 1/4-inch pieces with a knife dipped in water as you squeeze.

3 Return the saucepan to medium heat and bring almost to a simmer; do not boil. Cook over medium heat, removing the dumplings with a slotted spoon as they float to the surface; taste to be sure they are cooked through. Place in a bowl of cold water and reserve for soup.

Fish Dumplings
Fiskeboller

Serves 4 to 6 with soup

8 ounces cod or other
    white fish fillets
Salt to taste
2 egg whites
1/2 cup all-purpose flour
1/2 cup heavy cream
1/8 teaspoon white pepper
1/2 teaspoon salt

1 Sprinkle the fish lightly with salt and let stand for 5 minutes to draw out some of the moisture; pat dry with paper towels. Combine the fish with the egg whites, flour, cream and white pepper in a food processor or blender and process to form a smooth dough. Chill in the refrigerator for 15 to 20 minutes.

2 Spoon the dough into a large pastry bag without a tip. Add 3 inches water to a medium saucepan and stir in 1/2 teaspoon salt. Bring to a boil and remove from the heat. Squeeze the dough from the pastry bag into the saucepan, cutting into 1/4-inch pieces with a knife dipped in water as you squeeze.

3 Return the saucepan to medium heat and bring almost to a simmer; do not boil. Cook over medium heat, removing the dumplings with a slotted spoon as they float to the surface; taste to be sure they are cooked through. Place in a bowl of cold water and reserve for Tomato Soup* or Mock Turtle Stew*.

4 You can use frozen fish for this recipe, but be sure to thaw them completely before sprinkling them with salt.

Meat Dumplings
Kødboller

Serves 4 to 6 with soup

8 ounces pork shoulder or
    similar cut
1/2 cup all-purpose flour
1/2 teaspoon salt
1/4 teaspoon ground pepper
1 egg
1/3 cup 2% milk
1/2 teaspoon salt

1 Grind the meat as many times as needed for a very smooth texture. Combine with the flour, 1/2 teaspoon salt and the pepper in a bowl and mix well. Add the egg and milk, mixing well after each addition.

2 Spoon the meat mixture into a large pastry bag without a tip. Add 3 inches water to a medium saucepan and stir in 1/2 teaspoon salt. Bring to a boil and remove from the heat. Squeeze the dumplings from the pastry bag into the saucepan, cutting into 1/4-inch pieces with a knife dipped in water as you squeeze.

3 Return the saucepan to medium heat and bring almost to a simmer; do not boil. Cook over medium heat, removing the dumplings with a slotted spoon as they float to the surface; taste to be sure they are cooked through. Place in a bowl of cold water and reserve for soup.

Cream of Kale Soup
Grønkålssuppe

Serves 4 to 6

4 smoked ham shanks
2 quarts (about) water
3 cups (1/4-inch) potato cubes
2 cups (1/4-inch) carrot cubes
1 cup (1/4-inch) celery root cubes
1 cup (1/4-inch) leek slices
1/2 cup (1/4-inch) yellow
    onion cubes
1 teaspoon salt
1 large bunch kale, thick
    stems removed
6 tablespoons (3/4 stick) butter
3/4 cup all-purpose flour
1 cup heavy cream or half-and-half
1 teaspoon ground pepper

1 Combine the ham shanks with the water in a saucepan. Bring to a boil and reduce the heat. Simmer for 50 minutes. Add the potatoes, carrots, celery root, leeks and onion. Bring to a boil and reduce the heat. Simmer for 10 minutes longer, skimming off any foam that appears on the surface of the cooking liquid. Drain, reserving the ham shanks, vegetables and 8 cups cooking broth.

2 Fill a medium saucepan halfway with water and add the salt. Bring to a boil and add the kale. Reduce the heat and simmer for 8 to10 minutes. Drain in a strainer, discarding the cooking liquid. Chop the kale very fine in a food processor or put it through a grinder. The kale should measure about 1 1/2 cups.

3 Melt the butter in the saucepan used to cook the kale. Add the flour and cook over medium heat for 2 to 3 minutes, stirring constantly. Add the reserved 8 cups cooking liquid and bring to a boil, stirring constantly. Reduce the heat and simmer for 3 to 4 minutes.

4 Add the cream, kale and ground pepper. Return to a boil and reduce the heat. Simmer for 1 to 2 minutes or until heated through. Add the vegetables and return to a boil. Ladle into soup bowls and serve with the ham shanks, Bolted Rye Bread* or Pumpkernickel Bread* and Mustard*.

This mill was built in 1861 by Christian Sommer. It is located outside of Svaneke on the island of Bornholm.

Potato Leek Soup

Kartoffel og porresuppe

Serves 4 to 6

3 cups thinly sliced
   peeled potatoes
2 cups chicken stock
2 cups (1/4-inch pieces) potatoes
2 leeks, white portions only, sliced
4 cups chicken stock
6 tablespoons (3/4 stick) butter
3/4 cup all-purpose flour
1 cup heavy cream or half-and-half
1 1/2 teaspoons salt
1/2 teaspoon ground white pepper

1 Combine the sliced potatoes with 2 cups chicken stock in a small saucepan. Bring to a boil and reduce the heat. Simmer for 15 minutes. Remove from the heat; do not drain.

2 Combine the chopped potatoes, leeks and 4 cups chicken stock in a small saucepan. Bring to a boil and reduce the heat. Simmer for 12 minutes or until the potatoes are cooked through but still firm. Drain, reserving the cooking liquid.

3 Melt the butter in a heavy medium saucepan. Add the flour and cook over medium heat for 2 to 3 minutes, stirring until smooth. Add the reserved cooking liquid and bring to a boil, stirring constantly.

4 Mash the undrained sliced potatoes with the cooking liquid. Add to the sauce in the saucepan and mix well. Return to a boil and reduce the heat. Simmer for 2 minutes. Stir in the cream, salt and white pepper. Simmer for several minutes.

5 Add the chopped potatoes and leeks. Simmer for 1 minute. Ladle into soup bowls and garnish with leeks sautéed in butter. Serve with freshly baked White Bread*.

6 You can use a mixture of water and chicken base in place of the chicken stock or substitute mashed potatoes for the sliced potatoes.

Sue's Onion Soup

Sue's løgsuppe

Serves 4 to 6

3 yellow onions
1/4 cup (1/2 stick) butter
1/4 cup olive oil
1/2 teaspoon sugar
6 cups beef stock, or a mixture
   of 6 cups water and
   2 tablespoons beef base
2 bay leaves
1 teaspoon salt
1/4 teaspoon ground pepper
2 tablespoons dry sherry
Sliced French bread
1 1/3 to 2 cups grated Swiss cheese

I got this great soup from my wonderful wife, Sue.

1 Cut the onions into halves and then into thin slices. Heat the butter and olive oil in a heavy medium saucepan over low to medium heat. Add the onions and sugar and sauté over low heat for 20 to 30 minutes or until the onions are golden brown, stirring occasionally.

2 Add the beef stock, bay leaves, salt and pepper. Bring to a boil and reduce the heat. Simmer for 15 to 20 minutes. Stir in the sherry and discard the bay leaves.

3 Toast French bread under the broiler until golden brown. Ladle the soup into ovenproof soup bowls. Top each serving with a piece of toast and sprinkle 1/2 cup of the cheese onto each piece. Broil until the cheese is bubbly and brown. Place the hot soup bowls on serving plates and serve immediately.

Tomato Soup
Tomatsuppe

Serves 4

1 yellow onion
1/4 cup (1/2 stick) butter
1/2 cup all-purpose flour
2 (14-ounce) cans chicken stock
3 Roma tomatoes, finely chopped
1/2 teaspoon salt
12 peppercorns
1 (10-ounce) can tomato purée
1/4 cup heavy cream
1 leek, white portion only,
    very thinly sliced
1/2 tablespoon butter
1/2 recipe Fish Dumplings*

1 Sauté the onion in 1/4 cup butter in a heavy medium saucepan over
  medium heat for 5 to 8 minutes or until translucent. Add the flour and
cook for 2 to 3 minutes, stirring until smooth. Stir in the chicken stock and
bring to a boil, stirring constantly. Add the tomatoes, salt and peppercorns.
Simmer for 15 minutes.

2 Strain the mixture into a bowl, discarding the tomatoes, onion and
  peppercorns. Return the liquid to the saucepan and stir in the tomato
purée. Return to a boil and reduce the heat. Simmer for several minutes.
Add the cream and mix well; keep warm.

3 Sauté the leek in 1/2 tablespoon butter in a skillet for 3 to 4 minutes.
  Spoon the Fish Dumplings into the soup bowls and ladle the soup
into the bowls. Top with the sautéed leeks.

Cold Buttermilk Soup with Strawberries
Kærnemælkskoldskål med jordbær

Serves 4 to 6

1 1/2 cups fresh or frozen
    strawberries
3 tablespoons sugar
5 cups buttermilk
3/4 cup heavy cream
1/4 teaspoon vanilla extract
Toppings, such as cornflakes,
    Fruit Soup Biscuits*, whipped
    cream, vanilla ice cream
    and/or sliced fresh strawberries

*My favorite toppings for this are cornflakes, ice cream and, of course,
whipped cream.*

1 Combine the strawberries with the sugar and 2 cups of the buttermilk
  in a blender or food processor; process until smooth. Combine with
the remaining 3 cups buttermilk, cream and vanilla in a medium bowl;
mix well. Chill in the refrigerator for 1 hour or longer.

2 Ladle into soup bowls and top with cornflakes, Fruit Soup Biscuits,
  whipped cream, vanilla ice cream and/or sliced fresh strawberries.

3 You can mash the strawberries with a fork and then add the sugar
  and buttermilk if you do not have a blender or food processor.

Rhubarb and Raspberry Soup
Rabarber og hindbærsuppe

Serves 4 to 6

3 large ribs rhubarb
8 cups water
2 cups fresh or frozen raspberries
1 cup sugar
2 teaspoons vanilla extract
5 tablespoons cornstarch
1/2 cup cool water
3 cups fresh or frozen raspberries
1 recipe Fruit Soup Biscuits*

This also makes a great warm weather soup when chilled overnight and served cold. If it gets too thick in the refrigerator, thin it with a little apple juice or other juice. If the rhubarb is very young and tender, you can leave it in the soup with the raspberries.

1 Trim the rhubarb and cut the stems into 1/2-inch pieces, discarding the leaves. Combine with 8 cups water, 2 cups raspberries and sugar in a heavy medium saucepan; mix well. Bring to a boil and reduce the heat. Simmer for 30 minutes. Strain into a bowl, discarding the rhubarb and raspberry seeds.

2 Return the liquid to the saucepan and stir in the vanilla. Return to a boil. Blend the cornstarch with 1/2 cup water in a cup. Add to the saucepan and return to a boil, stirring constantly. Stir in 3 cups raspberries and reduce the heat. Simmer for 1 to 2 minutes. Adjust the sugar to taste. Ladle into soup bowls and serve with Fruit Soup Biscuits.

Desserts & Cakes

Desserter & Kager

Dessert is like an evening at Tivoli in Copenhagen! Dessert is fun, full of exciting conversation, laughter, and oohs and ahhs! Dessert is never missed, and I mean never!

Everyone must experience the Rødgrød med fløde. It is always a good laugh for Danes when an American English speaker tries to pronounce this one! But it is well worth the humiliation to indulge in the rich cooked berries and cream dish. Another fun tradition is Rice Pudding on Christmas Eve. We all dig to find the one and only whole almond in this traditional dessert. Whoever gets the almond wins the marzipan pig! This tradition dates back to the 1500s when the finder was given the right to kiss whoever he or she desired at the dinner party.

For birthday parties, the Layer Cake is a must whether it's a party for kids or adults. And who could resist the Marzipan Cake? It makes a stunning centerpiece for any occasion.

Trifle, bread pudding, pastries, and fine cakes—these are truly the finest tastes of Denmark.

Enjoy!

Trifle with Cake

Trifli med kage

Serves 10 to 12

1 (2-layer) package French vanilla
    cake mix

1^1/$_3$ cup water, at room temperature

^{1}/$_3$ cup vegetable oil

3 eggs

1 (5-ounce) package vanilla instant
    pudding mix

2^1/$_2$ cups cold 2% milk

Sweet sherry

5 cups (about) berries and fruit,
    such as strawberries,
    blueberries, raspberries,
    blackberries and/or peaches

3 cups (about) heavy
    whipping cream

It is best to bake the cake for this the day before serving. You can use any combination of berries and fruit, even individually quick-frozen berries and sprinkle the fruit with a little sugar if you like.

1 Combine the cake mix, water, oil and eggs in a medium mixing bowl and beat at low speed until combined. Beat at high speed for 2 minutes or until smooth. Spread in three lightly greased 8- or 9-inch cake pans. Bake at 350 degrees for 20 minutes or until the layers test done. Remove to a wire rack to cool.

2 Combine the pudding mix and milk in a small mixing bowl. Beat at medium speed for 2 minutes or until smooth.

3 Trim one of the cake layers about ^{3}/$_4$ inch to fit in the bowl. Place in a trifle bowl 8 inches in diameter and 5 inches deep. Sprinkle with sherry and spread with one-third of the pudding. Arrange one-third of the berries and fruit over the pudding.

4 Trim the remaining cake layers to fit the bowl. Repeat the layering process with the remaining cake layers, pudding and fruit. Whip the cream until firm peaks form. Spoon into a pastry bag and pipe over the top. Chill in the refrigerator for several hours before serving. Serve with additional whipped cream. Store in the refrigerator for several days.

Trifle with Macaroons
Trifli med makroner

Serves 4

1/2 recipe Macaroons*,
  about 10 macaroons
1 recipe Vanilla Cream Filling*
  (below)
2 teaspoons sweet sherry
Fresh fruit, such as raspberries,
  strawberries, blackberries,
  peaches and/or bananas
2 cups heavy whipping cream
2 tablespoons confectioners' sugar
Shaved chocolate

1 Prepare the Macaroons and Vanilla Cream Filling. Place one Macaroon in each of four dessert glasses and sprinkle each with 1/2 teaspoon sherry. Top each with 1/4 cup Cream Filling and a layer of fresh fruit.

2 Crumble six Macaroons and sprinkle over the fruit; top with the remaining Vanilla Cream Filling.

3 Whip the cream with the confectioners' sugar in a mixing bowl until soft peaks form. Spoon or pipe over the trifles and garnish with additional fruit and shaved chocolate. Chill in the refrigerator for 1 to 2 hours before serving. You can substitute thawed frozen fruit, drained canned fruit or Fruit Dessert* for the fresh fruit in this recipe.

Vanilla Cream Filling
Vanillecrem

Serves 4 to 6

3 egg yolks
2 tablespoons sugar
2 teaspoons vanilla extract
1 tablespoon cornstarch
2 cups heavy cream
1 teaspoon sugar

1 Mix the egg yolks and 2 tablespoons sugar in a medium mixing bowl until smooth. Beat in the vanilla and cornstarch. Bring the cream to a boil in a heavy medium saucepan, stirring constantly to prevent scorching. Add the cream very gradually to the egg yolk mixture, whisking constantly.

2 Return to the saucepan and bring to a boil, stirring constantly. Pour the mixture into a bowl. Sprinkle with 1 teaspoon sugar to prevent a skin from forming on the surface. Cool in the refrigerator. Use for Danish Birthday Cake*, Cookie Medallions*, Trifle with Macaroons* and other desserts.

Apple Charlotte

Æblekage

Serves 4

1 1/3 cups dry unseasoned bread
    crumbs
1/3 cup sugar
6 tablespoons (3/4 stick) butter
Sweet sherry
1 (24-ounce) jar home-style
    chunky applesauce
Whipped cream
Raspberry Jam*, cherries and/or
    shredded chocolate

1 Mix the bread crumbs with the sugar in a medium bowl. Melt the butter
in a skillet over medium heat; do not brown. Add the bread crumbs and
sauté until golden brown. Spoon into the bowl and cool.

2 Divide one-third of the bread crumbs evenly between four dessert
dishes and sprinkle lightly with sherry. Layer the applesauce and
remaining bread crumbs one-half at a time in the prepared dessert dishes,
sprinkling each bread crumb layer with sherry.

3 Chill in the refrigerator for 1 hour or longer before serving. Top with
whipped cream and decorate as desired with Raspberry Jam, cherries,
shredded chocolate and/or a Danish flag.

Bread Pudding with Brandy Sauce
Brødbudding med Cognac Sovs

Serves 6 to 8

Pudding

1 Granny Smith apple or other
   tart apple
6 cups (1/4-inch cubes) dry
   French bread
1 cup raisins
3 eggs
1 cup packed brown sugar
2 cups 2% milk
1 teaspoon vanilla extract

Sauce

1/2 cup packed brown sugar
1 1/4 cups water
1 teaspoon vanilla extract
1 1/2 tablespoons cornstarch
1/4 cup brandy or cognac
2 tablespoons butter

Pudding

1 Peel and core the apple and grate using the large holes of a grater. Combine with the bread cubes and raisins in a large bowl.

2 Beat the eggs in a bowl until frothy. Beat in the brown sugar. Add the milk and vanilla and mix well. Pour over the bread mixture and let stand for 15 minutes to absorb the liquid, stirring every few minutes.

3 Spoon into a generously buttered 8×8-inch baking pan. Place in a larger baking pan and add water to a depth of 1 1/2 inches. Bake at 375 degrees for 45 minutes or until a tester comes out clean.

Sauce

Combine the brown sugar, water and vanilla in a saucepan. Bring to a boil. Blend the cornstarch and brandy in a small bowl. Stir into the hot mixture and cook for 1 minute, stirring constantly. Remove from the heat and blend in the butter. Spoon over the hot pudding and serve with vanilla ice cream.

Tak for mad!

"Tak for mad" means thanks for the meal, or if it was a really great meal, you can say "Mange tak for mad," thank you very much for the meal. That is probably the most used sentence in the Danish language and would be the most important for a visitor to Denmark to learn.

As children, we were taught to say Tak for mad after every meal; it was usually one of the first sentences we learned. As adults, we use it at home and when visiting friends, and most visits are planned around a meal. It is good practice to say Tak for mad when the meal is over, and then when the evening is over, we shake hands with the hosting couple and say Tak for mad and a great evening.

Danish Cream Pudding

Fromage

Serves 8 to 10

1 ounce unflavored gelatin

1/4 cup cold water

3/4 cup sugar

3/4 cup water

4 eggs

4 egg yolks

3 3/4 cups heavy whipping cream, whipped

1 Sprinkle the gelatin over 1/4 cup cold water in a small cup and let stand for 1 minute or until softened. Bring the sugar and 3/4 cup water to a boil in a small saucepan, stirring to dissolve the sugar. Boil for 2 minutes. Add the gelatin and heat until the gelatin dissolves, stirring constantly.

2 Combine the eggs and egg yolks in a medium-large stainless steel mixing bowl. Place over simmering water and beat until smooth and warm. Remove from the water and gradually add the sugar syrup, whipping constantly until light and evenly fluffy. Whip until slightly cooled.

3 Fold half the whipped cream into the egg mixture one-fourth at a time. Fold the egg mixture into the remaining whipped cream. Spoon into a serving bowl or springform pan. Chill for several hours or until firm. Unmold onto a serving platter. Decorate with additional whipped cream and fruit or chocolate.

For **Rum Pudding (Romfromage)**, stir 1/2 cup rum into the mixture before folding in the whipped cream. You can use this pudding for the Rubinstein Cake*.

For **Lemon Pudding (Citronfromage)**, add an additional 1/4 ounce gelatin to the basic recipe. Stir 3/4 cup lemon juice and 1 teaspoon grated lemon zest into the mixture before folding in the whipped cream.

For **Orange Pudding (Appelsinfromage)**, add 1/2 ounce gelatin and 1 tablespoon cold water to the basic recipe. Stir 1 cup orange juice, 1/4 cup lemon juice and 1 tablespoon grated orange zest into the mixture before folding in the whipped cream. Color the mixture with several drops of orange food coloring or a mixture of yellow and red food coloring.

For **Chocolate Pudding (Chokoladefromage)**, stir 1 cup melted dark chocolate and 1/4 cup brandy into the mixture before folding in the whipped cream.

Rice Pudding
Ris á l'amande

If you have a goose down bed cover like we use in Denmark, you can cook the rice for about 15 minutes, then cover the saucepan with a dish towel and place it in the bed for about 3 hours. The rice will be cooked and you will have a warm bed to sleep in.

Serves 4 to 6

Pudding

2 tablespoons sugar
Pinch of salt
2 1/4 cups 2% milk
1 cup uncooked short grain
    pearl rice
2 tablespoons slivered almonds
1 cup heavy whipping cream
1/2 teaspoon vanilla extract
3/4 cup heavy whipping cream,
    whipped

Cherry Sauce

1 (16-ounce) can cherries
1/2 cup water
1 1/2 tablespoons cornstarch
1/4 cup Triple Sec (optional)

Pudding

1 Sprinkle the sugar and salt into the milk in a medium saucepan. Bring to a boil, stirring to prevent scorching. Stir in the rice and return to a boil. Turn the heat as low as possible and simmer for 50 to 60 minutes or until the rice is tender, but some liquid remains. Cool in the refrigerator for several hours to overnight. Stir in the almonds.

2 Whip 1 cup cream with the vanilla in a mixing bowl just until soft peaks form. Fold into the rice one-third at a time. Spoon into a serving bowl and top with 3/4 cup whipped cream. Garnish with fruit.

3 Add a whole almond to the pudding if it is to be served at Christmas. It is the holiday tradition to give a prize to the person who finds the almond.

Sauce

Drain the juice from the cherries and bring to a boil in a small saucepan. Blend the water and cornstarch in a cup. Add to the boiling juice and cook until thickened, stirring constantly. Add the cherries and liqueur. Return to a boil and serve with the pudding.

Rice Pancakes
Risklatter

Serves 4 to 6

1/2 recipe cold Rice Porridge*
2 eggs
3 tablespoons (or more)
    all-purpose flour
2 tablespoons sugar
1/4 cup raisins
2 tablespoons slivered almonds
Butter

1 Combine the Rice Porridge with the eggs in a large mixing bowl and mix well. Add the flour, sugar, raisins and almonds and mix well. Melt butter in a large skillet over medium heat.

2 Spoon the batter into the skillet by large spoonfuls. Cook for 2 minutes and turn the pancakes over. Cook for 2 minutes longer or until golden brown. Repeat with the remaining batter, adding flour if the batter becomes too thin. Serve with additional sugar and Raspberry Jam*. Serve as a dessert or snack.

Fruit Dessert

Rødgrød med fløde

Serves 4 to 6

3 cups fresh or frozen berries,
    a single kind or a mixture
    of berries

1 cup water or fruit juice other than
    orange juice

1/4 teaspoon vanilla extract

1/2 cup sugar

2 teaspoons cornstarch

1/4 cup cold water

1 tablespoon sugar

Milk, half-and-half or heavy cream

1 Combine the berries with 1 cup water in a saucepan and bring to a boil. Reduce the heat and simmer for several minutes. Stir in the vanilla and 1/2 cup sugar. Blend the cornstarch with 1/4 cup cold water in a small bowl. Stir into the berry mixture. Cook until thickened, stirring constantly. Reduce the heat and simmer for 1 minute.

2 Pour into a heat-proof bowl and sprinkle with 1 tablespoon sugar to prevent a skin from forming. Cover and chill in the refrigerator. Ladle into bowls and garnish with milk, half-and-half or cream. Sprinkle with additional sugar, if desired.

3 Serve as a dessert or healthy snack. You can reserve 1 cup of the berries to add after the cornstarch if you would like some whole berries in the dessert.

Baked Brie
1 Brie cheese
Butter, softened
Sliced or slivered almonds

Deep-Fried Brie
1 Brie cheese, or wedge of
    Brie cheese
1 egg, beaten
Bread crumbs
Vegetable oil for deep-frying

Danish Brie
Dansk Brie

Use a young Brie cheese for these recipes, as a ripe Brie will melt too fast. You can use a wedge of Brie to deep-fry, but you need a large Brie to bake. A Danish Camembert can also be used. Serve these as a dessert with a glass of Port, as a snack with crackers and a glass of red wine, or as part of a smorgasbord.

Baked Brie
Spread the top of the cheese with butter and sprinkle generously with almonds. Place in a small baking pan. Bake at 425 degrees on the center oven rack for 15 to 20 minutes or until the almonds are golden brown.

Deep-Fried Brie
Dip the cheese into the egg and coat with the bread crumbs. Repeat the process to coat thickly. Add enough oil to a small saucepan to cover the cheese. Heat the oil to 350 degrees on a thermometer or until it sizzles a wooden pick. Add the cheese carefully to the oil and deep-fry for 5 to 6 minutes or until golden brown. Drain on a paper towel and serve immediately.

Serves 4

2 1/4 cups whole milk
1 1/2 cups heavy cream
3/4 cup buttermilk
6 slices Pumpkernickel Bread*,
    dried and grated
Brown sugar

Dessert Milk
Tykmælk

My mom always covered the bowls of tykmælk with an inverted plate so she could stack them several high. With six boys, that came in handy!

1 Combine the milk and cream in a medium saucepan. Bring almost to a boil over medium to high heat, stirring constantly; do not boil. Cool to 80 degrees or about room temperature. Stir in the buttermilk.

2 Pour into individual serving bowls and cover with plastic wrap. Let stand at room temperature for 14 to 24 hours; the mixture will have the consistency of yogurt. Chill in the refrigerator for 1 or 2 hours before serving. Top with the grated Pumpernickel Bread and brown sugar. Serve as a dessert or snack.

Serves 7

Waffles

1 cup (2 sticks) butter, chopped
1 cup unbleached bread flour
1/4 cup water
Sugar crystals

Butter Cream

1/2 cup (1 stick) butter, softened
3/4 cup confectioners' sugar
2 teaspoons vanilla extract

French Waffles

Franske vafler

Franske vafler are also referred to as "øretæver," which translates as "box on the ear."

Waffles

1 Combine the butter and flour in a large mixing bowl and mix with a spoon. Add the water and beat with an electric mixer just until smooth; do not overmix. Shape into a ball and wrap with plastic wrap. Chill in the refrigerator for 1 hour or longer.

2 Roll the dough 1/4 inch thick on a lightly floured surface. Pierce holes in the dough with a fork and cut into circles with a 3-inch cutter. Sprinkle a sheet of baking parchment with sugar crystals. Place one dough circle at a time upside down on the baking parchment and roll into a 3×6-inch oval.

3 Arrange seven ovals on each of two lightly greased 12×17-inch baking pans, placing the sugar side up. Place one pan at a time on the center oven rack and bake at 450 degrees for 8 to 10 minutes or until light golden brown.

Butter Cream

Combine the butter, confectioners' sugar and vanilla in a bowl and mix with a spoon until smooth. Spread the mixture over half the waffles at serving time and top with the remaining waffles. You can also fill the waffles with whipped cream. Store unused waffles in an airtight container for several days.

Pastry Pretzel Kringle

Serves 10 to 12

Dough

4¼ cups unbleached bread flour
2 tablespoons instant dry yeast
2 tablespoons granulated sugar
1 cup plus 2 tablespoons
　　(2¼ sticks) butter, softened
3 eggs, beaten
¾ cup cold water

Filling

½ cup (1 stick) butter, softened
½ cup granulated sugar
½ cup finely chopped Macaroons*
⅓ cup almond paste
½ cup raisins

Topping

1 egg, beaten
2 tablespoons sugar crystals
⅓ cup whole almonds,
　　coarsely chopped

Dough

Mix the flour, yeast and sugar in a large mixing bowl. Add the butter and mix well. Beat in the eggs. Add the water and mix to form a dough. Knead on a lightly floured surface for 5 to 7 minutes or until smooth and elastic. Shape into a ball and let stand for 10 minutes. Roll the dough into a strip 4 feet long and 5 inches wide.

Filling

1 Cream the butter and sugar in a mixing bowl until light and fluffy. Mix in the Macaroons. Grate in the almond paste using the large holes of a grater; mix until smooth.

2 Spread down the center of the dough and sprinkle with the raisins. Fold over one side of the dough over the filling to just past the center of the strip. Fold over the other side to overlap a little and seal loosely.

3 Line a 12×17-inch baking pan with baking parchment and spray lightly with nonstick cooking spray. Place the baking pan close to the dough strip and slide it gently onto the pan, shaping it into a pretzel shape. Top with plastic wrap sprayed with nonstick cooking spray. Let rise at room temperature for 1 hour.

Topping

Brush the top with egg and sprinkle with half the sugar crystals. Sprinkle with the almonds and the remaining sugar crystals. Place on the center oven rack and bake at 400 degrees for 22 to 24 minutes or until golden brown. Cool on the baking pan for 1 hour. Decorate to suit the occasion and serve with hot chocolate topped with whipped cream.

Wienerbrød

Although the translation of the name for Danish pastry is Wienerbrød, the word translates literally as Viennese bread. The recipe for this style of pastry dough was first used in Vienna, Austria, back in the early 1800s and was introduced to Denmark in the middle of that century by Austrian bakers who had moved to Denmark. It has been further developed by Danish bakers and is now the wonderful Wienerbrød pastry we all love, with its crisp buttery layers in so many shapes and forms. It is a real treat for visitors to Denmark, but a little hard to copy in a home kitchen.

Rubinstein Cake
Rubinsteinerkage

Serves 10 to 12

1 recipe Macaroon Cake Layer*
1/2 cup Raspberry Jam*
1 recipe Rum Pudding*
1/2 cup granulated sugar
1 cup milk chocolate pieces
1/2 recipe small Cream Puffs*
1 cup heavy whipping cream
2 tablespoons confectioners' sugar
1/2 teaspoon vanilla extract

1 Place the Macaroon Cake Layer on a 12-inch serving plate and spread the center with Raspberry Jam. Place the ring of a 9-inch springform pan on the Macaroon Cake Layer and spoon the Rum Pudding into the ring, filling almost to the top and reserving the remaining pudding for the Cream Puffs. Chill in the refrigerator for several hours or until the pudding is set.

2 Melt the granulated sugar in a small saucepan over medium heat, stirring until the sugar is caramelized. Pour onto a sheet of baking parchment to cool. Melt the chocolate in a double boiler.

3 Cut the Cream Puffs into halves and fill the bottoms with the reserved Rum Pudding. Dip half the tops into the melted chocolate and drizzle melted chocolate on the other half. Replace on the bottoms and place on a tray lined with baking parchment.

4 Whip the cream in a mixing bowl until soft peaks form. Add the confectioners' sugar and vanilla and whip until firm peaks form. Spoon into a pastry bag.

5 Remove the chilled pudding layer from the refrigerator and remove the springform ring. Pipe the whipped cream over the top and arrange the Cream Puffs on and around the dessert. Break the caramelized sugar into pieces and sprinkle on the top. Garnish with chocolate shavings.

Macaroon Cake Layer
Makronlag

Makes 1 layer

1 cup almond paste
1 1/2 cups confectioners' sugar
2 egg whites

1 Grate the almond paste into a medium mixing bowl using the large holes on a grater. Add the confectioners' sugar and beat at low speed until well mixed and crumbly. Add the egg whites gradually, mixing until smooth.

2 Line a 12×17-inch baking sheet with baking parchment. Draw an 8-inch circle on the parchment. Spoon the batter onto the circle and spread with a spatula to fill the circle. Place on the center oven rack and bake at 400 degrees for 12 to 14 minutes or until golden brown.

3 Cool on the baking sheet on a wire rack; the cake layer will fall slightly as it cools. Use as the base layer for Danish Birthday Cake* or Rubinstein Cake*.

Cream Puffs

Vandbakkelser

Makes 30 medium cream puffs

2 cups water
1 cup (2 sticks) butter
1/2 teaspoon salt
2 cups unbleached bread flour
8 or 9 (2 cups) eggs
1 (5-ounce) package vanilla
    instant pudding mix
2 1/2 cups milk
2 cups heavy whipping cream,
    whipped
1/4 cup confectioners' sugar
1/2 teaspoon vanilla extract
Raspberry Jam*

1 Combine the water, butter and salt in a heavy medium saucepan and bring to a boil, stirring to melt the butter. Add the flour and cook over medium heat, stirring constantly with a wooden spoon until the dough leaves the side of the saucepan.

2 Remove to a bowl to mix with an electric mixer or leave in the saucepan to mix by hand. Beat in the eggs one at a time, mixing until the dough is smooth and shiny. Use two teaspoons, a small ice cream scoop or a pastry bag fitted with a star tip to drop the dough onto a 12×17-inch baking pan lined with baking parchment.

3 Place one baking pan at a time on the center oven rack and bake at 430 degrees for 12 minutes. Reduce the oven temperature to 375 degrees and bake for 30 to 35 minutes or until crisp on the top; underbaked cream puffs will fall as they cool. Remove to a wire rack to cool.

4 Combine the pudding mix with the milk in a bowl and beat until smooth. Whip the cream with the confectioners' sugar and vanilla in a bowl until soft peaks form.

5 Cut the cream puffs into halves and spoon a large teaspoonful of the pudding into the bottom halves. Top with a small teaspoonful of Raspberry Jam and the whipped cream; replace the top halves of the cream puffs. Garnish with a sifting of confectioners' sugar or baking cocoa over the tops.

6 This can also be used for other desserts, such as éclairs, miniature cream puffs, and Rubinstein Cake*.

 Marzipan

Both the Italians and the Germans claim to be the inventor of marzipan, for which there are recipes dating back to the Middle Ages. With the help of marzipan, almond paste was created in Denmark, and the kransekage is the centerpiece of weddings, birthdays, New Year's Eve celebrations and many other special occasions.

Marzipan Cake
Kransekage

Serves 10 to 12

Cake

2 pounds almond paste
2 cups confectioners' sugar
3 egg whites

Icing

1 egg white
1¹/4 cups confectioners' sugar

Rings forms are available to shape the rings for kransekage, but they are difficult to find and hard to use.

Cake

1 Grate the almond paste into a large saucepan using the large holes on a grater. Add the confectioners' sugar and mix by hand to form a very sticky dough; wear gloves if desired to help with the stickiness. Add the egg whites and heat over low heat just until warm enough to incorporate the egg white with your hands. Cool the dough to firm it up again.

2 Line 12×17-inch baking sheets with baking parchment. Draw a circle 6¹/2 inches in diameter on the baking parchment. Draw additional circles decreasing each circle ¹/2 inch in diameter. The smallest circle should have a diameter of 2 inches.

3 Roll the dough into ropes with a diameter of ¹/2 inch. Cut the ropes into sections and shape into rings on the drawn circles, pressing the ends to seal. Pinch the tops to make slightly triangular. Use any leftover dough to form pieces for decoration. Bake at 460 degrees on the center rack for 7 to 8 minutes or until light golden brown. Cool on a wire rack.

Icing

Beat the egg white with the confectioners' sugar in a mixing bowl until stiff peaks form. Spoon into a pastry bag fitted with a fine tip or a cone made from rolled baking parchment with the tip cut off. Pipe over each ring and let stand until the icing is firm and dry. Assemble the cake, starting with the largest circle and ending with the smallest. Decorate to suit the occasion.

Danish Birthday Layer Cake

Føselsdagslagkage

Serves 10 to 12

1 1/3 cups unbleached bread flour

1 teaspoon baking powder

3/4 cup (1 1/2 sticks) butter, softened

1 cup granulated sugar

3 eggs

3 tablespoons 2% milk

3/4 cup Raspberry Jam*

Vanilla Cream Filling*

2 cups heavy whipping cream

1/4 cup confectioners' sugar

1/2 teaspoon vanilla extract

1 Mix the flour with the baking powder. Cream the butter and granulated sugar in a medium mixing bowl until light and fluffy. Beat in the eggs one at a time. Add the flour mixture and mix well. Add the milk gradually, mixing until smooth.

2 Line three 12×17-inch baking sheets with baking parchment. Draw an 8-inch circle on each. Spoon the batter onto the circles and spread to fill the circles evenly. Bake at 435 degrees on the center oven rack for 8 to 10 minutes or until light golden brown. Remove to wire racks to cool for several hours.

3 Remove one cake layer to a serving plate and spread with the Raspberry Jam. Spread one layer with the Vanilla Cream Filling and place it on the first layer. Top with the remaining cake layer.

4 Whip the cream in a mixing bowl until frothy. Add the confectioners' sugar and vanilla and whip until firm peaks form. Spoon into a pastry bag and pipe over the cake. Decorate with flags and candles for a birthday or with chocolate-dipped strawberries, raspberries and shaved chocolate for other occasions.

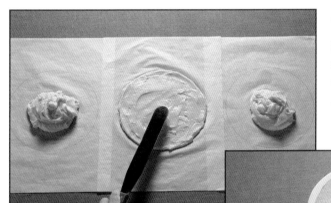

Layer Cake the Easy Way
Lagkage

Serves 12

1 (2-layer) package French vanilla
  cake mix
1¹/₄ cups water
¹/₃ cup vegetable oil
3 eggs
1 (5-ounce) package vanilla instant
  pudding mix
2¹/₂ cups 2% milk
1 cup Raspberry Jam*
4 cups heavy whipping cream
¹/₂ cup confectioners' sugar
1 teaspoon vanilla extract

I developed this recipe for a layer cake that is a little easier than making the layers for a true Danish Birthday Cake. In Denmark, you can even buy the layers in the market! For the best results, bake the cake one day in advance and let stand overnight. Fill and layer the cake several hours before decorating. Be sure to use a good-quality whipped cream that will hold up, or you can frost it with a simple icing if you prefer.*

1 Prepare the cake mix with the water, oil and eggs using the package directions. Bake in a 12×17-inch cake pan lined with baking parchment. Combine the pudding mix with the milk and prepare using the package directions.

2 Cut the cooled cake horizontally into three layers. Place the first layer on a serving platter and spread with about 2 cups of the pudding (you can eat the rest of the pudding). Spread the Raspberry Jam on the second layer and place on the pudding layer. Top with the third layer.

3 Whip the cream in a mixing bowl until soft peaks form. Add the confectioners' sugar and vanilla and mix until firm peaks form. Spoon into a pastry bag and pipe over the top and sides of the cake. Store in the refrigerator for up to 4 days.

Danish Flag Cake

Dannebrogskage

Serves 12

12/3 cups unbleached bread flour
11/2 teaspoons baking powder
1 cup (2 sticks) butter, softened
1 cup granulated sugar
2 eggs
1/3 cup 2% milk
1 teaspoon vanilla extract
12 strawberries, cut into halves
1/2 cup (about) strawberry glaze
2 cups heavy whipping cream
1/4 cup confectioners' sugar
1/2 teaspoon vanilla extract

This cake is traditionally served on May 5, the Danish Constitution Day—Grundlovsdagen—and therefore it is also referred to as Constitution Cake, or Grundlovskage. Naturally, it can also be served on other special occasions.

1 Mix the flour and baking powder in a bowl. Cream the butter and granulated sugar in a large mixing bowl until light and fluffy. Beat in the eggs one at a time. Add the flour mixture gradually, stirring to mix well after each addition. Stir in the milk and 1 teaspoon vanilla; do not overmix.

2 Spoon into an 8×11-inch cake pan sprayed with nonstick cooking spray. Place on the center oven rack and bake at 400 degrees for 15 minutes. Reduce the oven temperature to 375 degrees and bake for 15 minutes longer or until the cake tests done with a wooden pick. Cool in the pan on a wire rack for 30 minutes. Invert onto a serving tray to cool completely.

3 Arrange the strawberries on four sections of the cake to resemble the Danish flag, or Dannebrog. Top the strawberries with the strawberry glaze. Whip the cream in a mixing bowl until soft peaks form, adding the confectioners' sugar and 1/2 teaspoon vanilla. Spoon into a pastry bag and pipe around the edges and between the strawberries.

Ice Cream – Flødeis

Ice cream is an important part of the Danish culture. Being a dairy land it produces some of the best ice cream in the world—rich and creamy. In the summertime you will see the ice cream stands everywhere selling delicious ice cream cones and ice cream bars. They are expensive but well worth the price.

The ice cream is even more popular in Greenland who has the highest consumption of ice cream per capita in the world. When I worked at a hotel in Greenland the most popular dessert we could serve the employees was ice cream!

Pound Cake

Sandkage

Serves 8

1 cup plus 6 tablespoons
(2³/4 sticks) butter, softened
1¹/2 cups sugar
5 eggs
2 cups unbleached bread flour

If you translate the name Sandkag directly, it means sand cake.
Be careful not to overbake it, or it will become just that! It makes
a great strawberry shortcake.

1 Cream the butter and sugar in a large mixing bowl until light and fluffy. Beat in the eggs one at a time. Add the flour and mix with a spoon just until incorporated.

2 Spoon into a 5×9-inch baking pan sprayed with nonstick cooking spray. Place on the center oven rack and bake at 350 degrees for 1 hour or until a wooden pick comes out clean.

3 Cool in the pan on a wire rack for 15 minutes. Remove from the pan to the wire rack and cool for 15 to 20 minutes longer before slicing.

Marble Pound Cake – Marmorkage
For a marble pound cake prepare the batter for a pound cake, removing
one-third of the batter to a small mixing bowl. Add ¹/3 cup baking
cocoa to the small bowl and mix well. Spoon one-third of the white batter
into the prepared baking pan and spread with the chocolate batter.
Top with the remaining white batter and stir slightly with a wooden pick
to mix. Bake as for the pound cake.

Breakfast Cake

Brunsviger

Serves 6 to 8

3 cups unbleached bread flour

3 tablespoons granulated sugar

4 teaspoons instant dry yeast

1/2 teaspoon ground cardamom

3/4 teaspoon salt

3 tablespoons unsalted butter

1 1/3 cups 2% milk

10 tablespoons (1 1/4 sticks)
    unsalted butter, melted

1 cup packed brown sugar

2 teaspoons pancake syrup

1/3 cup packed brown sugar

1 Mix the flour with the granulated sugar, yeast, cardamom and salt in a mixing bowl. Combine 3 tablespoons butter with the milk in a microwave-safe bowl and microwave to 85 degrees. Add to the flour mixture and knead with the dough hook attachment or by hand for 4 to 5 minutes or until smooth and elastic.

2 Place in an oiled bowl, turning to coat the surface. Cover and let rise in a warm place for 30 minutes. Press the dough into an oiled 9×13-inch baking dish.

3 Mix 10 tablespoons butter, 1 cup brown sugar and the syrup in a small bowl. Spread the mixture over the dough. Press indentations in the dough with your fingers and sprinkle with 1/3 cup brown sugar. Cover the dough and let rise at room temperature for 20 minutes.

4 Place on the center oven rack and place a larger baking pan on the lower oven rack to catch any brown sugar spills. Bake at 375 degrees for 25 minutes. Cool in the pan on a wire rack. Cut into squares to serve.

Chocolate Frangipane
Chokolademandelkage

Serves 10

Cake

6 tablespoons unbleached
   bread flour
6 tablespoons baking cocoa
7 ounces almond paste
$1/2$ cup granulated sugar
$1/2$ cup (1 stick) butter, softened
3 eggs

Topping

4 ounces milk chocolate
2 tablespoons heavy cream
2 tablespoons ($1/4$ stick) butter
2 tablespoons confectioners' sugar
Raspberries (optional)

Cake

1 Mix the flour and baking cocoa together. Grate the almond paste into a medium mixing bowl using the large holes on a grater. Add the granulated sugar and butter and beat at low speed until combined. Beat at high speed for 2 to 3 minutes or until smooth. Beat in the eggs one at a time. Sift in the flour mixture, folding gently to mix evenly.

2 Spoon the mixture into a greased and floured 9-inch tart pan and spread evenly. Place on the center oven rack and bake at 350 degrees for 25 minutes or until set on the edge, but still a little sticky in the center. Cool on a wire rack. Remove to a serving plate.

Topping

1 Combine the chocolate with the cream and butter in the top of a double boiler. Heat over simmering water until the chocolate and butter melt, stirring to blend. Pour over the cooled cake and spread evenly.

2 Blend the confectioners' sugar with a few drops of water in a small cup. Spoon into a cone of rolled baking parchment and cut off the tip. Pipe over the cake in a decorative pattern. Arrange raspberries around the edge. Let stand for several hours before serving.

Raspberry Roll
Hindbærroulade

Serves 18 to 20

1 cup unbleached bread flour
$1/2$ teaspoon baking powder
$3/4$ cup ($1 1/2$ sticks) butter,
   softened
$3/4$ cup sugar
3 eggs
$3/4$ cup Raspberry Jam*

1 Mix the flour and baking powder together. Cream the butter and sugar in a mixing bowl until light and fluffy. Beat in the eggs one at a time, scraping the bowl after each addition. Add the flour mixture and mix until smooth.

2 Spread the batter evenly in a 12×16-inch baking pan lined with baking parchment, leaving a 1-inch edge on all sides. Place on the center oven rack and bake at 460 degrees for 6 to 7 minutes or until set.

3 Invert the cake onto a baking parchment sprinkled with sugar. Remove the parchment from the bottom of the cake and spread the cake evenly with the Raspberry Jam. Roll the cake tightly from the long side to enclose the jam, using the baking parchment to assist in rolling. Wrap in the baking parchment and let stand for 10 to 15 minutes before slicing.

Cookies

Småkager

You have probably tried the famous Danish Butter Cookies in the tins that are available all over the world. They are great, but nothing can beat freshly baked cookies from authentic Danish recipes. They're well worth your time and trouble.

The Danish word for Cookies, Småkager, is translated as "Small Cakes". That is really how they started, the bakers taking small pieces of cake dough and placing it in the oven for testing the temperature of the oven. Most of these recipes date back to the 1800s when ovens first started to become standard equipment in most kitchens, but the Deep Fried Cookies, Klejner, can be tracked back to the 1600s.

Traditionally these cookies are baked at Christmastime, but they are also a welcome addition to a cup of coffee or tea any time of the year. So turn on the oven, choose a recipe, and get baking!

Aristocrat Cookies
Aristokrater

Makes 27 or 28

1³/4 sticks butter, chopped
    and softened
3/4 cup sugar
1²/3 cups unbleached bread flour
1/3 cup chopped almonds
1/2 egg
1/2 tablespoon vanilla extract

1 Cream the butter with the sugar in a medium mixing bowl until light and fluffy. Add the flour, almonds and egg and mix well, first with the mixer and then with the hands, to form a smooth dough.

2 Shape the dough into a roll 2 inches in diameter and wrap in plastic wrap. Press the roll lightly to shape it into a square. Chill in the refrigerator for 1 hour or longer for ease of slicing.

3 Cut the roll into 1/4-inch slices. Arrange on a 12×17-inch cookie sheet lined with baking parchment. Place on the center oven rack and bake at 475 degrees for 8 to 10 minutes or until light golden brown. Remove to a wire rack to cool. Store in an airtight container for up to 2 weeks.

Brown Cookies
Brune kager

Makes 45 to 50

3 cups unbleached bread flour
1/8 teaspoon baking soda
1/2 teaspoon ground cardamom
1 teaspoon ground cinnamon
1 teaspoon ground cloves
1¹/4 sticks butter
1 cup plus 2 tablespoons packed
    brown sugar
1 egg
2/3 cup maple syrup or
    pancake syrup
1 cup water
50 whole almonds
1 egg
2 tablespoons water

1 Mix the flour, baking soda, cardamom, cinnamon and cloves together. Cream the butter with the brown sugar in a large mixing bowl until light and fluffy. Mix in the egg and syrup. Add the dry ingredients and mix well with a spoon. Chill in the refrigerator for 1 hour.

2 Bring 1 cup water to a boil in a small saucepan. Add the almonds and reduce the heat. Simmer for 50 to 60 seconds. Drain the almonds and press between two fingers to remove the skins.

3 Roll the dough 1/8- to 1/4-inch thick on a lightly floured surface. Cut with a 2¹/2- to 3-inch cutter and arrange on a 12×17-inch cookie sheet sprayed with nonstick cooking spray. Brush with a wash of 1 egg beaten with 2 tablespoons water and top each cookie with an almond.

4 Place on the center oven rack and bake at 425 degrees for 7 to 9 minutes or until firm. Remove to a wire rack to cool. Store in an airtight container for up to 3 weeks.

Cookie Medallions

Medaljer

Makes 18 to 20

Cookies

1 cup confectioners' sugar
2³/4 cups unbleached bread flour
1 cup (2 sticks) butter, chopped
1 egg
1 cup (about) Raspberry Jam*
1 recipe Vanilla Cream Filling*

Icing

¹/2 cup confectioners' sugar
2¹/2 teaspoons boiling water
¹/2 cup confectioners' sugar
1 tablespoon baking cocoa
3¹/2 teaspoons boiling water
Jelly, maraschino cherries and
     colored sugar crystals

Cookies

1 Sift the confectioners' sugar into a large mixing bowl and add the flour; mix well by hand. Add the butter and egg and mix with your hands to form a smooth dough. Chill in the refrigerator for 1 hour.

2 Roll the dough ¹/4 inch thick on a work surface. Cut into circles with a 2³/4-inch cutter. Arrange on a 12×17-inch cookie sheet sprayed with nonstick cooking spray. Place on the center oven rack and bake at 425 degrees for 7 to 8 minutes or until the cookies are set but not brown. Remove to a wire rack to cool.

3 Spread a layer of Raspberry Jam on half the cookies and top with a tablespoon of Vanilla Cream Filling*. Top with the remaining cookies.

Icing

Blend ¹/2 cup confectioners' sugar with 2¹/2 teaspoons boiling water in a bowl for white icing. Spread over half the cookies. Mix ¹/2 cup confectioners' sugar with 1 tablespoon baking cocoa in a bowl and stir in 3¹/2 teaspoons boiling water for chocolate icing. Spread over the remaining cookies. Top the cookies with jelly, maraschino cherries or colored sugar crystals.

Hygge

Hygge is truly a Danish word that is part of Danish life and the national character, but it is a word that is hard to translate. If you look it up in a dictionary, you will see that it translates as comfort or coziness, but it is much more than that! It is about feelings, emotions, being relaxed and secure. Hygge is often associated with food when family and friends gather to eat a smorgasbord for hours. It is associated with Christmas when you enjoy a big meal or just a hot red wine toddy with some Christmas cookies. For people planning to visit Denmark, there really should be a school where you could learn the concept of hygge.

Deep-Fried Cookies

Klejner

Makes 28 to 30

1/3 cup sugar
1/8 teaspoon baking soda
1 teaspoon ground cardamom
1/4 cup (1/2 stick) butter, chopped
    and softened
1 egg
1 tablespoon 2% milk
12/3 cups unbleached bread flour
Vegetable oil for deep-frying

1 Mix the sugar, baking soda and cardamon in a medium mixing bowl. Add the butter and mix until smooth. Blend in the egg and milk. Add the flour and mix first with a spoon and then with your hands to form a dough. Let stand for 10 minutes.

2 Roll the dough 1/8 inch thick on a work surface. Cut the dough into strips 1 1/4 inches wide with a knife or pizza cutter. Cut the strips diagonally into 3-inch pieces. Cut a 1 1/2-inch slit lengthwise in each piece. Place one corner of each piece through the slit and pull the dough to stretch it.

3 Heat the oil to 350 degrees in a deep-fryer or heavy saucepan. Test the oil with a thermometer or wooden pick; when the oil sizzles around the pick, the oil is ready.

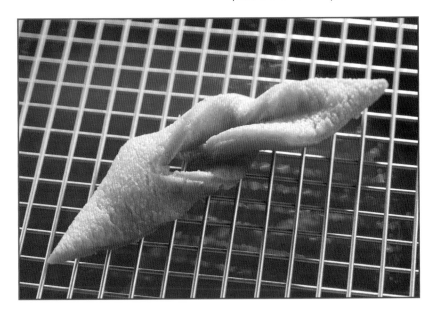

4 Add four or five of the twists at a time carefully to the hot oil. Deep-fry for 2 to 2 1/2 minutes or until golden brown, turning the cookies after 1 1/2 minutes. Drain on paper towels and cool slightly. Store in an airtight container for several days. These are great Christmas cookies.

Hot Spiced Wine – Gløgg

Gløgg is traditionally served at Christmastime and is often served with Danish doughnuts, or æbleskiver. To make four to six servings, mix 1 bottle of dry red wine with 1 1/2 cups port, 1 cup raisins, 1/2 orange peel, 1/2 cinnamon stick and 1/16 teaspoon ground cardamom in a stainless steel saucepan. Let the mixture stand overnight. Stir in 2 tablespoons sugar and bring just to a simmer over high heat; do not boil or the alcohol will evaporate. Stir in 1/4 cup Grand Marnier and 1/2 cup slivered almonds. You can add 1/4 cup aquavit, if desired. Serve hot with a spoon in cups.

Lemon Ring Cookies
Citronkranse

Makes 32 to 35 cookies

3/4 cup (1 1/2 sticks) butter, chopped and softened
3/4 cup sugar
Grated zest of 1 lemon
1 2/3 cups unbleached bread flour
1 egg

This recipe suggests shaping the dough into long rolls in a meat grinder. You can just as easily shape the dough into rolls by hand if you don't have the correct equipment or if you just don't want to go to the trouble of cleaning it.

1 Cream the butter and sugar in a medium mixing bowl until light and fluffy. Add the lemon zest, flour and egg and mix first with the mixer and then by hand to form a smooth dough.

2 Run the dough through a meat grinder fitted with the sausage tube to shape it into long rolls or shape into long thin rolls by hand. Cut the rolls into 4-inch pieces and shape into circles, pressing the ends to seal.

3 Arrange the rings on a 12×17-inch cookie sheet lined with baking parchment. Place on the center oven rack and bake at 475 degrees for 8 minutes. Remove to a wire rack to cool. Serve with a glass of port. Store in an airtight container for up to 2 weeks.

Macaroons
Makroner

Makes 20

7 ounces almond paste
1 cup confectioners' sugar
2 tablespoons unbleached bread flour
1/4 cup egg whites
1/4 teaspoon vanilla extract

Measure the egg whites carefully to ensure success. Any more than 1/4 cup will make macaroons that look like pancakes.

1 Grate the almond paste into a medium mixing bowl, using the large holes on a grater. Add the confectioners' sugar and flour and mix at medium speed until the mixture is crumbly.

2 Beat the egg whites in a small mixing bowl until frothy. Add the vanilla. Add to the crumb mixture gradually, mixing constantly at medium speed. Increase the speed to high and beat for several minutes until smooth and creamy.

3 Use a small ice cream scoop or two teaspoons to drop the dough onto a 12×17-inch cookie sheet lined with baking parchment, leaving room for the cookies to expand. Place on the center oven rack and bake at 350 degrees for 12 to 15 minutes or until light golden brown.

4 Remove to a wire rack to cool; the cookies will fall slightly as they cool. These cookies can be used to make Trifle with Macaroons*.

Butter Macaroon Cookies

Smørmakroner

Makes 40

3/4 cup (1 1/2 sticks) butter,
    chopped and softened
1 1/4 cups confectioners' sugar
1 3/4 cups unbleached bread flour
1 egg
1/8 teaspoon baking soda
1/2 cup coarsely chopped almonds
    or hazelnuts
1/2 cup raisins

1 Cream the butter and confectioners' sugar in a medium mixing bowl until light and fluffy. Add the flour, egg and baking soda and mix well. Add the almonds and raisins and mix well with a spoon.

2 Divide the dough into two portions and shape each portion into a roll 1 inch in diameter. Cut each roll into 3/4-inch pieces. Arrange the pieces on two 12×17-inch cookie sheets lightly sprayed with nonstick cooking spray. Press lightly to flatten.

3 Place on the center oven rack and bake at 450 degrees for 8 to 10 minutes or until light golden brown. Remove to a wire rack to cool. Serve with a glass of sweet sherry. Store in an airtight container.

Coconut Macaroons

Kokosmakroner

Makes 14 to 16

3 1/2 ounces almond paste
1 cup confectioners' sugar
1 1/2 cups sweetened
    flaked coconut
2 egg whites
1/2 teaspoon vanilla extract
1 cup (6 ounces) milk
    chocolate chips

1 Grate the almond paste into a medium mixing bowl using the large holes on a grater. Add the confectioners' sugar and mix at low speed until crumbly. Beat in the coconut.

2 Beat the egg whites in a small bowl until frothy. Add the vanilla and beat until soft peaks form. Fold into the coconut mixture, mixing well.

3 Line two 12×17-inch cookie sheets with baking parchment and spray the parchment with nonstick cooking spray. Use a #40 ice cream scoop or two spoons to scoop twelve cookies onto one cookie sheet. Continue scooping the remaining cookies onto the second cookie sheet.

4 Place on the center oven rack. Bake at 325 degrees for 16 to 18 minutes or until light golden brown. Remove to a wire rack and cool for 1 hour or longer.

5 Melt the chocolate chips in a double boiler over simmering water. Spread the chocolate over the bottoms of the cooled macaroons and let stand upside down until the chocolate is firm.

Meringue Cookies
Marengs

Makes 34 to 36

4 egg whites, at room
    temperature
2/3 cup granulated sugar
1 cup confectioners' sugar
1/2 cup baking cocoa (optional)

1. Beat the egg whites in a medium mixing bowl until fluffy. Add the granulated sugar gradually, mixing constantly at high speed until stiff peaks form; the egg whites are ready when you can turn the bowl upside down and the egg whites stay in the bowl.

2. Sift the confectioners' sugar and baking cocoa into a bowl. Fold into the egg whites gradually. Spoon the mixture into a pastry bag. Pipe into mounds 1 inch wide and 1 inch thick on a 12×17-inch cookie sheet lined with baking parchment.

3. Place on the center oven rack and bake at 225 degrees for 55 to 60 minutes or until the outside is crisp and the center is still slightly moist. Remove to a wire rack to cool for 1 hour. Store in an airtight container for up to 2 weeks.

4. Take care that none of the egg yolks are mixed with the egg white when you separate the eggs.

Peppernut Cookies
Pebernødder

Makes 110 to 120 very small cookies

2 1/2 cups unbleached bread flour
1 cup packed brown sugar
1 teaspoon ground nutmeg
1/2 teaspoon ground cardamom
1/4 teaspoon ground cloves
1/2 teaspoon ground pepper
1 cup (2 sticks) butter, chopped
    and softened
1 egg

1. Mix the flour, brown sugar, nutmeg, cardamom, cloves and pepper with a spoon in a medium bowl. Add the butter and egg and mix well with an electric mixer. Shape into a smooth dough with your hands. Chill in the refrigerator for 30 minutes.

2. Shape the dough into long rolls 1/2 inch in diameter. Cut the rolls into 1/4-inch slices and shape each slice into a small ball about the size of a hazelnut. Place on a 12×17-inch cookie sheet sprayed with nonstick cooking spray.

3. Place on the center oven rack and bake at 350 degrees for 12 minutes; do not allow to brown. Cool on a wire rack. Store in an airtight container for several weeks.

Sugar and Almond Cookies
Finskbrød

Makes 30

1²/₃ cups unbleached bread flour

¹/₂ cup granulated sugar

³/₄ cup (1¹/₂ sticks) butter,
chopped and softened

1 egg

2 tablespoons water

1¹/₂ tablespoons sugar crystals

¹/₃ cup finely chopped almonds
or hazelnuts

1 Mix the flour and granulated sugar in a mixing bowl. Add the butter and mix well first with a spoon and then with your hands to form a dough. Shape into a ball. Roll into a square ¹/₄ inch thick on a work surface. Cut into 1-inch-wide and 2-inch-long pieces with a knife or pizza cutter.

2 Beat the egg with the water in a small bowl. Brush over the dough; sprinkle with the sugar crystals and almonds. Arrange on a 12×17-inch cookie sheet sprayed with nonstick cooking spray.

3 Place on the center oven rack and bake at 425 degrees for 10 to 12 minutes or until light brown. Remove to a wire rack to cool. Serve with a glass of milk or Gløgg*. Store in an airtight container for several weeks.

Biscotti
Italienske Biscotti

Makes 22 to 24

1²/₃ cups unbleached bread flour

¹/₂ teaspoon baking powder

1¹/₃ cups sugar

1 cup whole almonds

7 ounces marzipan

3 eggs

2 teaspoons vanilla extract

1 Mix the flour, baking powder and sugar in a large mixing bowl. Stir in the almonds. Grate the marzipan into the bowl using the large holes on a grater; mix well. Beat the eggs with the vanilla in a small bowl. Add to the marzipan mixture and mix with gloved hands to form a sticky dough.

2 Shape into two rolls with a diameter of 1¹/₂ inches, using plastic wrap to shape the dough. Place in a 12×17-inch baking pan lined with baking parchment and remove the plastic wrap. Place on the center oven rack and bake at 350 degrees for 25 to 30 minutes. Remove to a wire rack and cool for 1 hour or longer.

3 Reduce the oven temperature to 325 degrees. Cut the loaves into ³/₄-inch slices and arrange cut side down in the baking pan. Bake at 325 degrees for 10 to 12 minutes or until lightly toasted. Serve with coffee, tea or hot chocolate for dunking. Store in an airtight container for several weeks.

Hot Wine Toddy – Varm rødvinstody
Hot Wine Toddy is a popular Danish drink on a cold winter evening. Mix 1 cup of merlot or other red wine with 2 tablespoons brandy and 2 tablespoons sugar in a 16-ounce mug or heavy glass. Add ³/₄ cup boiling water and stir to mix well. Cut an orange wedge between the peel and the flesh and place on the rim of the mug. Serve with Butter Macaroon Cookies or Sugar and Almond Cookies*.*

Porter's Dog Biscuits

Porter's hundekiks

Makes 44 to 48

2¹/₂ cups whole wheat flour
2¹/₂ cups unbleached bread flour
¹/₃ cup cracked wheat
2 tablespoons brown sugar
1 teaspoon salt
3 eggs
1 cup vegetable oil
¹/₄ cup au jus mix or
    bouillon cubes
1 cup hot water
1¹/₃ cups dry milk powder

This recipe was created in honor of our dog Porter. He is an American Eskimo, so he is not very Danish, but he likes these cookies!

1 Mix the whole wheat flour, bread flour, cracked wheat, brown sugar and salt in a large mixing bowl. Add the eggs and oil and mix well. Dissolve the au jus mix in the hot water in a small bowl and stir in the milk powder. Add to the flour mixture and mix to form a dough.

2 Knead until smooth and elastic, adjusting the flour or water as needed for a very firm dough. Cover the dough and let stand for 15 to 20 minutes. Roll ³/₈ inch thick on a work surface and cut with a 1¹/₂×3-inch bone-shaped cutter.

3 Arrange on 12×17-inch baking pans lined with baking parchment. Place on the center oven rack and bake at 350 degrees for 30 to 35 minutes or until firm and dry. Cool on a wire rack and store in an airtight container 5 to 6 feet from the floor!

Index

Indeks

To order additional books, please send $34.95 per book
plus $4.95 postage and handling to:

Cooking Danish
Stig Hansen
P.O. Box 930
Eden, Utah 84310-0930
(801) 745-0388

Utah residents, please add 6.6% sales tax.

Make checks or money orders payable to Stig Hansen.

For credit card orders, overseas orders or more information,
please visit the Web site at www.cookingdanish.com.